THE WILL TO WIN

THE WILL TO WIN

LEADING, COMPETING, SUCCEEDING

ROBERT HERJAVEC

with John Lawrence Reynolds

HarperCollins Publishers Ltd

Published by HarperCollins Publishers Ltd.

First Edition

HarperCollins Publishers Ltd
2 Bloor Street East, 20th Floor
Toronto, Ontario, Canada
M4W 1A8

www.harpercollins.ca

Library and Archives Canada Cataloguing in Publication
information is available upon request.

ISBN 978-1-44340-986-5

Printed and bound in the United States

RRD 9 8 7 6 5 4 3 2 1

To the memory of my parents,
who gave me love, support
and the opportunity to live my life in Canada.

To my wife, Diane,
whose presence in my life makes sharing our success
worth all the effort and energy.

To our children, Brendan, Skye and Caprice,
who carry my love and support with them
into their own bright and shining future.

And to all of those individuals who nurture a dream
and summon the courage to make it happen.

All good is hard. All evil is easy.

Dying, losing, cheating and mediocrity are easy.

Stay away from easy.

—Scott Alexander

CONTENTS

1

The Satisfaction Exceeds the Sacrifice

I must do about 100 media interviews across Canada and the United States each year, or maybe it just seems that way. Doing interviews is part of who I have become, thanks to my appearance on network television. It's not a chore to be asked about my background or my views on life by a reporter or talk-show host, but the glamour wore off long ago.

I don't resent doing interviews. In the words of travelling salesmen from a couple of generations ago, they come with the territory. But there is a limit to how much I can say about myself and to the subject the interviewers can ask about, so the questions are often both similar and familiar.

One interview a few months ago took me by surprise, however. It was especially interesting because it was for an automotive magazine. The first few questions focused on my racing experiences, as I expected. Then the interviewer pointed out that the first thing I listed on one of my media biographies had nothing to do with my auto racing activities or business career or TV appearances. "Your bio lists 'dad' and 'husband' ahead of any of your other identities," he said. "What does that say about you?"

It was a great question. "It says," I told him, "that as busy as I may get, I always take time for my family. I may not have what people call a balanced life, meaning I'm not home for dinner every night at the same time. But my kids know I'm always there for them, and that whatever else I may be doing, they are my first priority. The things I have achieved in my life are only of full value to me when I can share them with my family."

> **" The things I have achieved in my life are only of full value to me when I can share them with my family. "**

Later, after I thought about the interviewer's question, I wondered if I had chosen "dad" to be the first identity in my biography as a subconscious tribute to my father, whose life and relationship to his family were very different from my own. My dad arrived from Yugoslavia with a wife, an eight-year-old son and about 20 bucks in cash, and I suspect he had never been happier in his life than the first morning he woke up in Canada. Despite all the challenges, including being able to speak almost no English, he considered himself fortunate.

The first job he had—the only one he could get—was sweeping a factory floor. The better-paying jobs went to English-speaking, educated people, and many of them looked down on the immigrant pushing a broom. My dad didn't care. Back in Croatia he had been jailed more than 20 times for daring to speak his mind, and warned that one more charge could see him imprisoned for years. Here he was free not only to criticize the government but also to build whatever kind of life for himself and his family he chose. He was thankful for that opportunity his entire life—so thankful that he did something that other people thought was really foolish.

After several years of working in the factory, he was laid off. Okay, it happens. What he had to do, friends told my dad, was apply for unemployment insurance. It wouldn't bring in a lot of money, but it would carry us until he was rehired at his old job or found an entirely new one.

Dad refused to collect the benefits owed to him. He said he would find a way to get by until he was back at work again.

"But you paid into it," everyone told him. "It's there to help you out at a time like this. Take the money!"

He wouldn't touch it. "I'm lucky just to be here," he would say. "I don't need a handout from anybody. This country gave me a chance, and I'll make the most of it."

As far as I know, he didn't collect a penny of unemployment insurance. He found another job, resumed work and ignored the opportunity to take money for not working, which is the way he viewed the deal.

Was Dad stubborn? I guess he was, and in this case maybe he was foolish. He simply believed in taking responsibility for himself, and in sticking to his own principles, which included the idea that you collect a good day's pay for a good day's work. There is no reward for doing nothing, and the better you perform your job, the bigger the reward you receive. And if you fail to succeed, don't waste time blaming other people.

It's an old-fashioned idea maybe, but it's been at the heart of every job I've had. And it doesn't mean you can't have fun from the things you do, including your work. Hey, I want to enjoy every day of my life as much as I can, and I want the people around me to enjoy themselves as well. But I have found that the amount of enjoyment you get from anything you do is in direct proportion to the amount of effort you put into it.

I put a lot of effort into everything I do, including building my business in a highly competitive industry, racing my car against top-rated drivers, appearing on television to compete with Sharks and Dragons, trying to get my golf handicap down to the level I want and, yes, being the best possible dad to my children. I don't always succeed at the first four goals, but I refuse to risk failure at the last one.

Why try so hard? Well, why try anything unless you intend to win? Here's a hint: The best way of winning at anything is to enjoy competing.

"**There is no reward for doing nothing, and the better you perform your job, the bigger the reward you receive.**"

Not everything in life is restricted to just one winner. The World Series, the Super Bowl, the Stanley Cup playoffs and all the other sports competitions are set up to declare one winner, and that's fine. But life is different. If I can lower my golf handicap by three strokes this season, I've won. It doesn't matter who wins the Masters or the PGA Championship. In my personal competition, I'm a winner.

I know that if my company exceeds its targeted sales volume next year, it's a winner. And when I exchange high-fives with my kids about something they have accomplished on their own, and we laugh about it afterward, I'm definitely a winner. Even when

I don't finish in first place, I refuse to believe I lost. Given more time, I tell myself, I could have won. If nothing else, I learn how not to lose next time.

You don't need to be on television or on a racetrack or running a business to win at life. You need the determination to achieve everything that you're capable of doing, and the will to get it done. It's not all about sacrifices, by the way. Sure, sacrifices always need to be made if you've set goals for yourself and intend to meet them. But when you finally get it done and you've met your goals, the satisfaction always exceeds the sacrifice.

Always.

2

Why Get By on "Good Enough"?

I enjoy meeting people of all kinds from all walks of life. I especially enjoy meeting people who have realized great achievements despite the challenges they faced. You have to admire people with spirit—the ones who refuse to give up their dreams just because they are not as fast, not as strong, not as well-educated, or are lacking in some other vital quality compared with their competitors. I am never as impressed by people who *have* something—wealth or fame, for example—as I am by people who have *achieved* something, especially against great odds.

So I'm always a little surprised and disappointed when I meet people who have immense amounts of talent and ability yet never care enough to fulfil their promise. Hey, it's their life to live any way they please. But I will always believe that anyone who doesn't apply all of their talents to the fullest is squandering something valuable.

It occurs whenever someone fails to realize all of his or her potential by settling for less than they are capable of achieving.

Whether you want to build the next big company in communications technology, become the most respected teacher in your education system or have a lasting impact as an artist in your field, the most important decision you can make is to reject mediocrity. In the long run, "good enough" is never good enough, whether in our personal lives or in our careers. When we settle for "good enough," we never realize our capabilities. Even if you fail to grab the "golden ring," whatever it represents, take the risk and try, instead of playing it safe and never knowing if you could have achieved your dream.

I'm afraid that "good enough" has become too large a part of our culture. A mark of 50 percent in a school examination may be "good enough" to claim a passing grade, but unless it's accompanied by outstanding achievements in other subjects, it will never be good enough to win entry to a top university or launch a satisfying career with a successful company. This applies as much in the arts as it does in business.

> **" In the long run, 'good enough' is never good enough. "**

I have rented our house on two occasions to the Rolling Stones when they were in Toronto on a tour. This gave me the chance to watch Mick Jagger rehearse, work out, and generally take care of the band's business. Anyone who wonders how the Rolling Stones have managed to succeed over their 40-plus years of performing would understand after watching Mick Jagger at work. Aside from rehearsing every move he makes and every word he delivers, he invests hours each day maintaining his physical condition, watching his diet, and meditating. And it shows. Nearing 70, he still maintains enormous amounts of energy and focus. Walking away after watching him work, I thought to myself, "Boy, compared with Mick Jagger, I'm not that busy!"

Most fans of the Rolling Stones assume the band just goes out and has fun at every performance. They may have fun, but trust me—for every minute of fun on stage, they have invested an hour's worth of hard work preparing for it.

None of us can achieve perfection in everything we do, but all of us can be as good as our abilities enable us to be. So why should we settle for less than that? If you made it halfway to your goal and told yourself this was "good enough," would you be satisfied? If you were drowning 10 metres offshore and I threw a rope to you that landed 5 metres away, would that be good enough? After all, I could always claim that I met you halfway.

On the way to various finish lines I set for myself, I learned many lessons I want to share with you in this book. I also include tales of wisdom acquired from celebrities ranging from Oprah Winfrey to Georges St-Pierre. They may be special in some ways, but in other ways they are just like you and me. The difference is that none of them has ever settled for "good enough." And neither should you.

You can always do more.

A man who refused to waste his talent

We don't need to be perfectionists in everything we do—it's an imperfect world, after all. We do need, however, to do everything we are capable of doing in whatever pastime we choose. This is especially true when we possess a skill that sets us apart from others.

A writer friend once told me about a story he was preparing for a magazine. The story featured a group of musicians who gathered one evening a week in a local community hall to rehearse light classics—music that presented a moderate challenge to their abilities.

The orchestra members performed in public only three or four times a year, usually at charity events. Their musicianship was more than adequate, but none would ever make a serious challenge to play in the New York Philharmonic or the London Symphony, nor did they expect to. They knew the limits of their abilities, and they insisted on exploring them to those limits. Besides, each had a full-time career and other obligations beyond music, including family. Music was a passion and a pastime for them, not a profession. They took their practices and performances seriously, however, and their dedication was apparent in every concert.

Among the most intriguing of the musicians was a clarinettist whom the writer recognized as a highly regarded vascular surgeon. Along with attending to his demanding practice, the musician taught at a medical school and sat on advisory boards to address community health issues. This was a busy man, making significant contributions to society.

While practising a movement from Mozart's clarinet concerto during a rehearsal, the surgeon played with technical perfection and warm expression. Approaching him during a break, the writer asked, "How long have you been playing clarinet?"

"I started in high school," the doctor said.

"And do you come here every week?"

"I try to never miss a rehearsal. Or a performance."

"But why?" the writer asked. "You're busy with your medical responsibilities, your practice, your lectures and your other activities. And you must keep practising between rehearsals. Why spend so much time on your music?"

"If I didn't," he answered, "it would be a talent wasted."

The surgeon had no intention of becoming a famous musician. His chosen field was medicine, and he was obviously more than capable at it. But as long as he had a talent for music, he believed he should make the most of it, which is what he was doing. He could easily toss his music aside and claim, with much justification, that he had achieved success in his life. To dismiss his musical talent would have been easy and understandable. He chose not to waste his talent.

I like that story, and I think it illustrates three points.

First, anyone who becomes a highly skilled surgeon has already demonstrated enormous drive and dedication. If these are part of your psyche, as they are part of mine, you can't turn that stuff off. Some people would say, "I completed three surgeries and taught a class of students. That's enough for one day." It wasn't enough for the clarinet-playing doctor, and it was that attitude, I'm sure, that helped him become not just a surgeon but an *exceptional* surgeon.

Second, the most satisfying things we do in life have almost no connection with the money they provide us. The drama on *Dragons' Den* and *Shark Tank* may appear to be about money, and if the only Dragon or Shark you pay attention to is Kevin

O'Leary, you would become convinced of this. But it's not really true. The shows are about more than money, in my opinion. I never sought a penny of investment in launching and building my own companies. I could have, and perhaps there were times when I *should* have. But it never occurred to me because the pursuit of money was never my principle goal. Making money is still a secondary concern to me. It is more a means of measuring my success at something that I love to do. Like the clarinet-playing surgeon, I believe the best things we achieve in our lives are realized because we have both a talent and a passion to exercise that talent. Applying it to the best of our ability brings personal satisfaction that far exceeds the amount of money we earn from it.

And third, I'm confident that playing music with the orchestra each week aided the doctor in his medical practice. It would be a way of relaxing, of course, by shifting his mind away from one discipline to another totally different discipline. But I suspect it was more than that. I think he had more drive and ability than his medical practice and teaching could contain, and music provided a means of expressing it. One way or another, practicing and playing music made him a better surgeon. We all need release from the tensions of the day. Mine has been running, among other pursuits. The doctor's was playing clarinet.

" Applying our talent to the best of our ability brings personal satisfaction that far exceeds the amount of money we earn from it. "

I say this with some confidence because I have always wanted to make the most of certain skills and interests beyond my everyday activities. I get a lot of satisfaction and rewards from the business I founded in 2003. Building one of the fastest-growing companies in its field still gives me a rush. Within 10 years of being founded, the Herjavec Group has grown from three people in a single cramped office to 165 employees generating $125 million in sales and services, with offices in major cities throughout the country. My company has become the primary data integrator go-to name for clients across North America who demand high-quality Internet security, network and storage services.

Reaching well over $100 million in sales after just eight years was a major achievement, even in the high-flying technology industry. By comparison, it took 12 years for Oracle to hit $100 million and for Microsoft to reach just $50 million.

The Herjavec Group is the third business success in my career. I sold my first start-up firm in 2000, at the height of the dot-com bubble, and followed this with a successful turnaround of a Silicon Valley company. After spending a couple of years as a stay-at-home dad, growing close to our three children, until they were old enough to attend school full time, I was itching to return to business. More than return to it—I was driven to start an entirely new company with a unique focus.

My business success provided the time and the opportunity to engage in other things that appealed to me. I trained for and ran in marathons and resumed my interest in road racing. During the Ferrari Challenge road-racing season I compete against other drivers who are as determined as I am to do whatever it takes, within the rules, to win. Why do I risk my life, and a substantial amount of money, travelling at 300 kilometres per hour less than a metre behind the car in front of me? Because it's fun. And *because I want to win.* Winning at various challenges has enabled me to enjoy life in ways that would not be available to me without first achieving success in business.

The most dramatic recognition of my business success arrived with an invitation to become a member of the CBC television show *Dragons' Den,* where I sat with the original Dragons—Kevin O'Leary, Jim Treliving, Laurence Lewin and Jennifer Wood—judging, and sometimes investing in, people's entrepreneurial dreams. Later, W. Brett Wilson and Arlene Dickinson became Den residents. My appearance on *Dragons' Den* led to a similar role on the ABC TV show *Shark Tank,* and the chance to rub elbows with celebrities ranging from Oprah Winfrey and Celine Dion to Pitbull and David Foster.

Nothing I had done up to that point changed my life as much as participating in those two hit televisions shows. Working with immensely talented production people and entrepreneurs as driven as myself was always stimulating and usually great fun. The biggest impact, however, came with the national TV exposure and the way it catapulted me into celebrity status.

I had never intended to become famous in this manner, and it often surprised and even stunned me. I can't say I don't enjoy the experience. The most appealing part of recognition is the opportunity it provides to meet people I admire for their achievements both in and out of the limelight—people who, like me, are driven by their need to take their talents and abilities to the maximum level. Sharing our stories gives me a feeling of belonging because we have common interests and common goals. I love talking to them about the things they have achieved and the ambition that drove them to succeed, learning what makes them tick and hearing the challenges they overcame. One of the things I enjoy about being a celebrity is the feeling of belonging (whether it's based on reality or not) when meeting other successful people. I love talking to them, but I am not very good at approaching them on my own.

In September 2012, I surprised many people when I chose to leave *Dragons' Den* after six years on the show. I had been one of the original participants and had cemented friendships among the other Dragons, as well as among those within the industry.

Despite requests to discuss my reasons for leaving, I avoided interviews because I suspected that the interviewers would want me to say something negative about my decision. And I wouldn't. I have nothing negative to say. It was a great experience, but it's all in the past. I left with great memories, but beyond saying that, I have no other comments to make. Why? Because I am not good at looking at life through a rear-view mirror. My momentum is always forward, not backwards or sideways. *Dragons' Den* was great, but it's over.

Some people assumed I made the decision in order to focus on my role in *Shark Tank,* which, being a U.S. production, reaches several million more viewers than *Dragons' Den*. Or perhaps, they believed, it was to enable me to spend more time and energy on the racing circuit, hanging with the pit crews and searching for new tricks, new techniques to cross the finish line ahead of everyone else in the race.

The truth is, it was time to go. There are only 24 hours in a day, and while I love cars, golf and playing at all sorts of things, my business continues to grow at enormous speed. Every minute I spent focusing on one thing was a minute I was unable to spend on another. I was running out of time.

Between my business and my family, I couldn't do both shows. I needed to choose between them and, frankly, the U.S. show is more fun—not just for me but for my kids as well. We get invited to events like the American Music Awards, where my daughter got to hang out with Justin Bieber. *Shark Tank* is picking up more viewers with each show, to the point where the size of its Canadian audience is starting to rival the figures for *Dragons' Den* in Canada received. As I write this, *Shark Tank* has received an Emmy nomination and is about to launch its fifth season on ABC TV. In the ultra-competitive world of U.S. network television, scoring five consecutive seasons is a major achievement, and I'm proud to be part of it.

What's the best measure of success?

Never underestimate the value of having fun.

Whatever your age and whatever your financial status, if you wake up every morning determined to sample as much fun as possible, you will be wealthy in a special way. Having fun is the surest measure of success, and success, in my book, is defined as *doing what you want to do*. What's the purpose of working long hours if most of those hours are filled with tension? Life is to be enjoyed, and I enjoy almost everything I do each day, including the time and effort I dedicate to my work. My biggest source of fun involves tackling things I haven't done and finding ways to succeed at them. Don't get me wrong—sometimes there are really crappy days. I tell people, "If you don't have a really crappy day at work now and then, you just don't care enough!" There's a limit, of course. When the crappy days start to outnumber the really happy days, it's time to move on or rethink what you are doing. You cannot succeed at anything if you are miserable with yourself and your work.

I am not that different from you or anyone else in various measures, but the most important thing I have in common with people where business and life are concerned is this: *Everybody wants to be successful.* Everybody wants to finish first.

If this sounds like a simple-minded fact, you're right. No one with all their faculties intact has ever said, "I want to be a loser." Yet even while they are dreaming of success, many people find ways of avoiding it.

> " Even while dreaming of success, many people find ways of avoiding it. "

You don't have to be an entrepreneur or even a manager to understand and appreciate the idea of finishing first. In fact, you don't have to be in business at all. It's a matter of setting your own goals, growing determined to reach them and always searching for new goals to achieve. It's a matter of having the will to win. And it's a matter of applying that will to the thing that you enjoy doing most.

I enjoy my appearances on television. And I enjoy the competition of all-out auto racing. But I enjoy operating my business more. Launching and successfully operating my business

opened all the other doors in my life, and I never permit myself
to forget that. My business defines me and makes me who I am.
All the other stuff is fun and games.

3

The Secret to Successful Negotiating

Many people have asked me what's the difference between *Dragons' Den* and *Shark Tank*. Both are based on the same premise, both are hit shows building large audiences over time, both set up five business people as possible sources of investment for the participants, and both Kevin O'Leary and I have been on the two shows. So is one a carbon copy of the other?

Not really. *Shark Tank* has a strictly American angle to it, and it reflects the key difference, where business is concerned, between the United States and the rest of the world. The best comparison between *Dragons' Den* and *Shark Tank* is the atmosphere of the two shows; *Shark Tank* is definitely edgier. A level of tension exists on the set that viewers sense and that is missing in shows with a similar premise. All of us Sharks are deadly serious about snagging a good deal and leaving the others behind in a competitive atmosphere that is absolutely genuine. There is no posturing, no phony histrionics on the show. It's American-style free enterprise on display, with all of its raw competitiveness. More than once, *Shark Tank* producers have suggested that we all take a break and chill out before one of us begins throwing something besides angry words at another. The tense moments pass quickly, and usually we all get together after a taping session and relax, but a bit of residual friction often hangs in the air.

Part of this edgy nature is rooted in the Sharks themselves. Kevin O'Leary is just as his persona suggests: he assesses everything according to whether it will make money for him. In Kevin's book, anyone who seeks profit at Kevin's expense is greedy, and anyone whose business plan exhibits a flaw is a cockroach and will be crushed like one. Kevin has been hugely successful at raising his profile and establishing his unique brand, but I find his approach to life and his single-minded attitude toward money offensive.

To his credit, Kevin doesn't take criticism about his love for money above all else too seriously. I and other members of *Dragons' Den* were always able to tell Kevin he was acting like a jerk (sometimes using language far more colourful and insulting than that) and still go out and have a beer with him when the show was over.

Barbara Corcoran and Lori Greiner alternate as female Sharks, and they have more in common than their blonde hair colour. Both can be tough and aggressive, but I believe Lori is more confrontational. Some pitchers seeking an investment believe that Barbara or Lori will prove a softer touch than the men on the panel. Well, they may have softer voices, but they still demand answers, and they will cut off at the knees anyone who makes a poorly thought-out and badly presented pitch.

Daymond John has an urban street-smart manner that I find refreshing. When growing up in Brooklyn and Queens, his in-your-face attitude wasn't considered aggressive; it was just the normal way of doing things, and he maintains the approach with flashy bling and a high-fashion wardrobe. There is little subtlety to Daymond. When the cameras are on and the pitches are being assessed and the deals are being made, Daymond is all business. Off the set of *Shark Tank* he relaxes a little, and I'm probably closer to him than to the other Sharks. In fact, his children and mine are good buddies.

No one, however, epitomizes the unique atmosphere of *Shark Tank* better than Mark Cuban. When he was just 12 years old, Mark sold garbage bags door to door to raise money to buy some expensive basketball shoes, and he hasn't looked back since. Mark's favourite line is "What time is selling time? All the time!"

Something in the way Mark is wired urges him to keep selling, to keep amassing money without let-up. As wired as I may be to be driven, I'm not wired to that extent. There is a reason Mark is worth a billion dollars and I'm not—but I'm working on it!

As time has passed, the atmosphere between us on *Shark Tank* has grown more sharp, more in-your-face, yet I believe we're more comfortable and perhaps more honest with each other now. We have definitely become more cutthroat when it comes to grabbing at the chances to make money for ourselves. And it gets tougher every season.

Not every investment we make on *Shark Tank* earns a profit, but when it does, it can be big. The size of the potential returns on *Shark Tank* versus *Dragons' Den* marks one of the biggest differences between the two shows. The American market is 10 times the size of Canada's, so when you have a winner in the United States, it's often a *big* winner. That's why, although the really good investments are few and far between, when one of us spots an opportunity with a lot of promise, the knives come out and the attacks begin. Does this create real tension on the set? You bet it does.

So why do we stay on a show where it's so difficult to make money? For the same reason we all became entrepreneurs in the first place: To prove a point. To satisfy an itch. To beat the odds. And to find gold before someone else snatches it up. The profit, if and when it arrives, is a means of keeping score.

Three common errors people make when pitching for money

When I'm asked about the mistakes that people make when seeking investments on *Shark Tank,* I usually list three things.

First, too many pitchers are unrealistic about the value of their ideas or companies. Their valuations are far beyond the amount that the real world would accept. Knowing all of us Sharks have a good deal of wealth, they assume that we won't care much about the amount of money we're asked to risk on their ventures. Dumb move. They forget that we are Sharks because we *do* measure and watch how we spend our money, and are realistic about the profits we hope to earn from it. In many ways, we are not spendthrifts; we're tightwads.

The second mistake pitchers make on the show is failing to listen. I know they're nervous, and I know it's intimidating to stand in front of us and explain why their gizmos or companies can't fail, but they have to overcome their nervousness, listen carefully to our questions and understand our response to their answers. That's one way *Shark Tank* is very real. It deals with moments in the pitchers' lives that literally dictate their future, and they don't want to screw them up.

Their third mistake is that often they act like people looking for a handout. They need to act more like entrepreneurs. We're not on the show to award handouts. We're there to make investments, and among the things we look for on the part of those seeking an investment are passion and dedication. If we choose to invest in their concepts, we expect them to make our money work hard, and this can happen only if *they* work hard. If the people looking for our money are apathetic, or appear to be treating the process as a joke, they're probably not going to work as hard as possible to make their ideas successes. That's a deal-killer in itself. My dad often said that working hard doesn't guarantee you will be rich, but not working hard means you're sure to stay poor.

Thinking like a true entrepreneur means looking for the best possible deal, and very few of the people we encounter on *Shark Tank* do this. When the other Sharks and I see a deal that looks really good, with a product or service that promises growth and a sales record that has proven its value, we're prepared to battle each other for it. That's the whole premise of the show. Yet very few of the participants understand

> " Thinking like a true entrepreneur means looking for the best possible deal. "

how much they can gain by playing us off against one another.

I'm not offended when I make an offer and the person looking for my investment makes a counteroffer, as long as it's reasonable. I respect that person's business acumen when he or she
comes back at me this way. That's what all of us on *Shark Tank* do
day after day—look for the means to benefit from a better deal.
Participants should be reasonably aggressive in their counteroffer
without being greedy.

This controlled aggression is at the root of my success in many
endeavours, from growing a business and running marathons
to winning on the racetrack. "Aggression" doesn't mean the in-
your-face bullying of a Kevin O'Leary. It means an honest effort
to improve your status in a negotiation without offending the
person on the other side. The pitchers who appear on *Shark Tank*
need the same mindset. They need patience and the ability to read
each of us. It's not always easy, and it doesn't come naturally to
everybody. But those who learn and apply this mindset will fare
much better in business, and maybe in life.

4

A Lesson in Aggression

I didn't mind being called "the nice guy" among the Dragons and Sharks, but being nice doesn't mean I cannot be aggressive in business dealings or in any other aspects of my life when the situation needs it. I enjoy being kind to people, but don't mistake my kindness for cowardice. As a matter of fact, while writing this, I am aiming to grow more aggressive in various aspects of my life.

This adjustment begins with the way I act and drive on the racetrack, where I compete in the Ferrari 458 Challenge series of races each season. As its name indicates, the series is limited to Ferrari 458 models, thoroughbred race cars with an engine generating more than 560 horsepower and capable of going from zero to 100 kilometres per hour in about three seconds. To participate in the Challenge series, you must own a Ferrari 458 and race it yourself. This is not a spectator sport. You need more than money to participate. You need a total commitment to competing in a sport that involves the thrill of driving a thoroughbred race car at speeds approaching 300 kilometres per hour over race tracks and road circuits around the world. The 2013 racing schedule for me includes competing at sites around North America, plus, as part of the Maserati events, at tracks in Germany, France, China and the United Arab Emirates.

Am I serious about winning? You bet I am. By applying as much concentration to racing as I have to running my business, I managed to win the 2011 Rookie of the Year award on the last lap of the last race of the season, in Hollywood movie style.

It happened in Mugello, Italy, with two races remaining in the season. If I could finish in the top 15 for both of the races, I would be declared Rookie of the Year. I was pumped—but in the first race I got a flat tire and didn't finish. Now I needed to finish in at least fourth place or better to earn the points I needed. As the second race was winding up I was in fifth place, and on the final lap I passed the car ahead of me, scored a fourth-place finish and won the award.

Did it make the cover of *Sports Illustrated?* No, but it meant a huge amount to me because I had set a goal and achieved it.

No more waiting for a chance to pass the car in front of me

When I decided to compete in the Challenge series of races, I hired a coach to teach me the skills I needed. I had raced small sports cars in the past, but the Ferrari 458 Challenge is a whole other kind of competition, demanding a whole other set of driving skills.

For my coach, I chose a great guy named Tyler McQuarrie, a world-class driver who has scored his share of championship race wins. Tyler rides with me on practice laps and communicates with me through earphones during races, finding ways to save a tenth of a second on my lap times here, half a second there, over and over. That's how you make your way to the front in competitive racing: by seizing every opportunity to pass the car ahead of you, working your way to the front car by car and remaining there.

Thanks to Tyler's coaching, I managed to win the first of two races at the St. Petersburg Indy to launch the 2012 season, followed by wins at Laguna Seca near Monterey, California, and at Lime Rock in Connecticut.

The first win of the season at St. Petersburg was a real thrill, as you can imagine. I came off the track absolutely elated, proud of what I had achieved but unsure how much of it was simply due to good luck. Could I repeat the ride and win the next day's race as well?

Almost as soon as I climbed out of the car, Tyler told me we needed to talk.

"You did well," Tyler said when we sat down to discuss things. "You're a good driver, you're consistent in your approach and you listen to my advice. You're also running really fast laps." Then he grew very serious. "But the key to driving, remember, is not running the fastest lap. It's winning the damn race. And you've got a problem, Robert. You're not aggressive enough."

This was news to me. Of all the ways people have described me in my life, lacking in aggression has never been one of them.

I wanted to win as much as the next guy, in business and on the track. Me not aggressive enough? How could he possibly say that?

"You're driving faster," Tyler said, "and that's good. But as the speeds get faster, the reaction times get shorter, and that's where your problem lies. You have less time to make a decision when you're running at 200 kilometres per hour than you had at 180 kilometres per hour."

Okay, I understood that. I hadn't thought about it in detail, but I could grasp Tyler's point. So what?

"Here's what you are doing now," he went on. "When you come up on a car ahead of you in a race and you sit behind it, you're thinking. 'Wow! I've done it! I've caught this guy. Now I'll wait to see what he does wrong. When he makes a mistake, I'll try to get by him.' Isn't that the way you think?"

He was right. That was my mindset.

Was it so bad? Apparently it was.

"When you were running at last season's speed," Tyler explained, "that wasn't a real problem. But at the speed you are going now, you'll probably have one chance to get past the car ahead of you, and if you miss it, it'll be gone. So chances are that you won't pass him, which means you won't win the race."

He had made his point. Tyler, by the way, is one of the nicest guys you could ever hope to meet. He's friendly, easygoing and fun to kick back and hang out with when we're not racing. You need to remember this when hearing the rest of my story.

"Here's the way I think in a race," Tyler said, "and the way you have to think as well. When I come up on a guy ahead of me, I think, *'Get the hell out of my way! Why are you ahead of me? You do not deserve to be in my way! By being in my way you are taking victory out of my hands and food out of the mouths of my children! So get the hell out of my way!'* That's how I think in a race when somebody is ahead of me. And you need to think that way too."

I was stunned by his words. Sure, Tyler was competitive. Every race driver is, including me. But this was a side of Tyler I had never seen—or heard—before.

Seeing my shocked expression, Tyler added, "Let me explain to you. In a race, only one person can win, right? Once the race is over, I'm super nice. I'll have dinner with the guy who was ahead of me, I'll hang out with him, we'll have a few laughs and all of that. But once my racing helmet is on, the engine is running and the starter drops the flag . . . it's strictly *'Get the hell out of my way!'*"

Suddenly Tyler's attitude didn't seem so odd. He had described a state of mind similar to the one I have as a businessman.

"When you compete on a business deal," Tyler continued, "do you expect three of you to win on the same deal? I'll bet you don't."

He had nailed it perfectly. I have always told people in my company, "For us to win, somebody has to lose. When we win a sale, it means somebody else is losing a sale." So he was right. I had never articulated it in this manner, and certainly never said it aloud. But whenever I'm aiming at making a sales call or pitching a new customer, I look at my competitors just long enough to think, "*Get the hell out of my way!*"

Tyler's lesson was to adapt the same controlled aggression that I use in business to the racetrack. When I find a car ahead of me on the track, I shouldn't be wondering when the driver will make a mistake or how I will find a way of passing him before the race is over. The only thought that should enter my mind is a silent order: *"Get out of my way!"*

The next day, running in second place with a very fast car, I had a very good driver close on my tail. Tyler's words were still echoing in my head and, almost before I thought about it and faster than I could have predicted, I passed the car ahead of me, forcing the driver behind me to push himself and his car over the limit. When he spun out, my toughest competitors were behind me, and I won the race.

Back in the pits, feeling good about myself after scoring two wins in a row, I collared Tyler with a question. "Why," I asked him, "didn't you tell me all about this last year? Why wait until this year?"

"Because," Tyler said, "last year you were driving too slow. And you didn't know enough."

I understood. Before you can absorb the teachings of a master, you have to absorb a lot of advice and gather a lot of experience. Only then will you fully appreciate what the master is telling you and be able to apply it to your utmost advantage.

Sometimes you have to ease off on aggression

One more racing lesson:

Tyler's advice to me, and the general quality of his coaching, really paid off in that second race. It also revealed how much I had to learn.

With four laps to go, I remained comfortably in first place with a 10-second lead over the car behind me. Ten seconds doesn't sound like a very long time, but when travelling at high speed on a closed race course it's like an eternity to the drivers.

I was having the time of my life, constantly pulling away from the second-place car, when I heard Tyler's voice in my earpiece saying, "Don't overdrive the car."

I wasn't listening. I was 10 seconds ahead of everybody else, my car was humming and I felt terrific. In fact, I felt so good that I believed I could increase my lead by more than 10 seconds, so I ignored my coach's suggestion and began pushing the car even harder.

As usual, Tyler's voice of experience was right. Overdriving the car, forcing it beyond its limits, caused the tires to begin failing, and soon I was sliding all over the track, unable to maintain the precise line and speed that had put me in first place. I had to slow down substantially, and by the next lap I was just eight seconds ahead of the car behind me. On the next lap my lead was down to six seconds, and with two laps to go the second-place car was barely four seconds behind me. I managed to finish the race two and a half seconds ahead of the next car. That's an impressive lead, but had the race lasted another two laps or so, I wouldn't have won. Tyler had proved his point: Never overstress the car.

I understand the same lesson in a business context. There is no need to create urgency and pressure when all that's needed to win is to finish. In the end, winning is the only thing that matters. The number of seconds you may be ahead of the next guy or the number of points you score are secondary. A win is still a win, no matter how ugly it may be.

Why didn't I listen to Tyler's advice and avoid overdriving the car? Not because I didn't trust or believe him but because I had a problem dialing back my aggression.

Along with a valuable lesson about racing, I learned something about myself as well. Many of the things I do—participating in *Shark Tank,* running marathons and racing in the Ferrari Challenge series—are means of directing my aggression away from business. I know the danger of overdriving a business, pushing staff past the point of endurance and enthusiasm when the goal is already in sight. I can turn off the pressure on the people I work with, but I can't turn off the pressure within me that keeps pushing me to outperform everyone else, proving something to the world and maybe to myself as well.

> " There is no need to create urgency and pressure when all that's needed to win is to finish."

I learned that it's important under some circumstances to take things a little easier and avoid pushing things beyond their capabilities. Some business leaders push people beyond their limits as employees, resulting in less productivity and more staff dissatisfaction. Understanding the limits and being able to motivate people to work up to but not beyond these limits is one of the most valuable skills an employer can have.

Avoid mixing arrogance with aggression

I received another lesson when racing in Sonoma, California, in May 2012—one I shared with the world when footage appeared on YouTube, *Entertainment Tonight* and (at last count) about 2,000 other news outlets. I missed a curve and hit a wall—not at more than 200 kilometres per hour, as many media reports claimed, but fast enough to cause severe damage to the car. "How did it happen?" many people asked me. The answer was the difference between my determination to win ("Get the hell out of my way!") and my arrogance ("There is nothing about this car that I cannot handle!"). On the previous lap I had gone fast enough to qualify for second place, and I thought that with just one more lap I could go even faster and qualify for first place. Well, I couldn't. Highly tuned racing machines are capable of doing things at a far faster pace than the mind of even a trained and totally focused race driver can respond to. Racetrack crashes are rarely caused by the cars being unable to achieve what the driver asked of them. They're more likely caused by the driver being unable to recognize the limits of his or her ability to control the car.

In business, any time you make a mistake and it doesn't cost you money, you've just received a free lesson. In racing, any time you have a major crash and you can walk away unscratched, you've learned something you probably couldn't have learned from a book or a racing coach. Of course, in racing, you are also reminded of your own mortality, as well as the limits of your bank account, because fewer vehicles are more expensive to repair than a finely tuned Ferrari.

> " **In business, any time you make a mistake and it doesn't cost you money, you've just received a free lesson.** "

The value of commitment over technique

The crash at Sonoma created concern among some people. Why was I risking my life by racing down a track at speeds, in some cases, approaching 300 kilometres an hour, wheel to wheel with another car? Couldn't I find something else that was just as satisfying but did not involve so much danger?

I'm not sure I could. Besides, just how much risk was I taking? It all depends on how you measure it.

In business, I often look back at deals I made several years ago—companies I bought, contracts I signed, that sort of thing—and I ask myself, "How could I ever have taken that kind of risk? What was I thinking?" And the answer is: "It didn't seem risky at the time."

One of the keys to being a successful entrepreneur is being able to make decisions with the best data available at the time. You never have all the data you would like, or all the comfort level you would prefer, before going forward. Doesn't matter. When you're ready you push the throttle, get in the race and make it work. The risks we take depend on who we are and what we know at the time. This holds for business every bit as much as it does for racing.

> " The risks we take depend on who we are and what we know at the time. "

The decision to make a risky move depends on what you are doing and how well you are doing it at the time, and the people who grow worried when they hear about my involvement in motor car racing usually know very little about the sport. They assume that everyone gets behind the wheel of the car and drives as fast as possible to get to the finish line. That's true, but it's also like saying baseball consists of nothing but hitting a ball and running around the bases before somebody can throw the ball home. It's far more complex than that, and so is racing, especially where risk is concerned.

The Ferrari 458 Challenge race series is held on two kinds of tracks. One kind involves much shifting into lower gears to handle the tight curves. This means using a lot of technique and understanding the necessary mechanics involved in getting the car around the circuit in the shortest possible time. The other kind of track is generally raced in the highest possible gear and at the highest possible speed. Winning on this kind of track doesn't involve technique as much as it demands total commitment when approaching a corner at high speed.

By "commitment" I mean refusing to obey the message that your mind sends to your body, which is basically "Slow down!" Disregarding your instinct isn't essential just to win the race; it's essential to avoid disaster. Lifting your foot off the accelerator when turning into this kind of corner at high speed can make the car dangerously unstable. The laws of physics dictate that an unstable machine operating at or near its capacity becomes unpredictable, and unpredictable race cars are driven by drivers who become intimately acquainted with walls.

> **"Disregarding your instinct isn't essential just to win the race; it's essential to avoid disaster."**

Some drivers have a serious problem racing on tracks that favour commitment over technique. Approaching a corner at 200-plus kilometres per hour, they can't believe that they have to maintain or even increase their car's speed to make it through the corner safely and ahead of other cars, especially if missing the turn means making contact with a wall.

When I talk about this need for commitment to people unfamiliar with racing, they grow even more concerned. "How can you do that?" they ask. "Isn't that dangerous? Don't you have to be a little crazy to speed up instead of slowing down when you approach a corner?"

And I usually reply, "Are you kidding? The really crazy guys are the ones who try to do the same thing on a motorcycle. Now *that's* insane!"

I don't know how motorcycle racers would respond to my comment, although they might mention something they think is even riskier than their sport. It doesn't matter. We all have different ways of dealing with risk, and we all tolerate different levels of it. We simply need to know what those levels are and stay within the limits.

Usually.

5

The Moral of the Kodak Cow

Like most people of my generation, I was saddened to hear of the bankruptcy of Eastman Kodak in early 2012. When I was growing up, Kodak owned the photography business. Most people had a Kodak camera in their house for snapshots, and top professional photographers swore by Kodak film. Back in 1976, when "taking pictures" meant first buying the right kind of film you needed, loading it into the camera, removing it when finished and having it processed in a laboratory, Kodak owned 90 percent of the market. No matter who made your camera, nine out of 10 times it was loaded with Kodak film.

And there was more. The pictures were usually printed on paper made by Kodak, using chemicals manufactured by Kodak and processed on equipment designed by Kodak. Kodak was the Microsoft of its day. If you wanted to take pictures, you became a Kodak customer one way or another. As long as people wanted to take pictures, Kodak's future appeared solid.

That was the expectation. Here's the reality: starting around the year 2000, Eastman Kodak began its slide from being a giant to becoming a shell of a business that is unlikely, even if it survives economically, to be more than a sideline player in an industry it once dominated as much as any company in history dominated its industry.

Obviously, something went terribly wrong at Kodak. When the rest of the world shifted from light-sensitive film to digital memory as a means of taking pictures, Kodak ignored it. It's too bad, I thought, that the people at Kodak didn't jump aboard the digital bandwagon earlier. Were they blind to the advance of technology? How long had they ignored that technology? Why didn't they look into it earlier and keep up with the rest of the world?

Boy, was I surprised.

I discovered that Kodak had not ignored digital photography at all—Kodak had invented it!

Back in 1975, a young Kodak engineer began experimenting with something called a charge-coupled device, or CCD, which had been invented a few years earlier. He developed a system that let CCDs store images flashed onto them, performing the same task that light-sensitive film had been doing for about 100 years. Once the image was stored it could be manipulated into, among other things, data that a printer could use to put the image onto paper.

The people at Kodak weren't dumb. They knew the potential of this idea and patented it immediately. Then they sat down to decide what to do about this new invention. And that's when they blew it, in my opinion.

Kodak made billions of dollars each year from manufacturing and processing celluloid film. Its entire empire was built around that end of the business. Now it owned the basis for revolutionizing the industry. It would be like General Motors or Toyota switching from building cars to building aircraft, or Coca-Cola dropping soft drinks to become a dairy company. They could do it . . . but should they?

Kodak had the technology, the market position, the patents, the distribution network and the awareness that the future of photography would be based on digital technology and not on celluloid film. It had the cash to finance the technology shift, a global dealer network to distribute the products and, among casual users of cameras, the highest brand recognition and trust in the business.

What did Kodak lack? Confidence—in itself, its product, its capability and its brand. Management seems not to have believed in the company's ability to make the move to digital that everyone knew was both necessary and inevitable. Instead of reinventing the company as a key player with technology it had helped develop, Kodak chose to maximize its income on celluloid film for as long as it could. Let other companies make the investment and take the risk of moving to digital.

> " What did Kodak lack? Confidence—in itself, its product, its capability and its brand. "

Kodak would shift its attention from photography to copying machines. Apparently, it did a good job in that field. Kodak machines were considered the elite in their area, but the copier business alone couldn't support a company as large as Kodak.

That's the long explanation. The short explanation, in my view, is this: Kodak chickened out.

The company feared doing something it had never attempted before, and clung to both out-of-date technology and an ineffective means of creating a strategy for dealing with this kind of situation.* The people at the top of Kodak could see that digital cameras were going to take several years to grow as popular as film cameras and would need a large investment at the beginning. They also realized that digital technology, if sufficiently developed and successfully marketed, would eventually doom their film business. Even though the company pioneered the technology, Kodak decided to bury it, perhaps having fooled themselves into believing that no one would solve the technological challenges and digital would simply fade away.

That's the tale tossed around by business commentators, but I suspect there may be more to it. I wonder if Kodak management was more concerned about scoring enough return on the next quarter's earnings report to pump up their profit-based bonuses than about keeping the company alive and solvent.

It's difficult to make long-term decisions when you are aiming to deliver short-term gains every quarter. This kind of strategy may work for a while, but reality always has a way of catching up to you. I'm sure some people at Kodak looked far enough ahead to warn that the end of the road was in sight, and that the people at the top replied, "Yeah, we know, but let's just get past this next exit first," meaning the next

---

* Details on this event can be found at tech.fortune.cnn.com/2012/01/18/the-kodak-lie/.

quarterly financial report. In any case, Kodak feared making the move that would be necessary to maintain and even enhance its position as a leader in the industry, and it cost the company dearly.

Many people—including some top Kodak executives, I expect—would object to my use of the word "fear" in describing what happened to the company. They might prefer "caution" or "restraint." They might even settle for "miscalculation." But I call it fear. And while it's unusual to apply the word to an entire corporation, especially one as once-dominant and aggressive as Kodak, fear is indeed common among managers and entrepreneurs at every level.

" **Fear is indeed common among managers and entrepreneurs at every level.** "

I understand fear. If I'm walking alone in the woods and round a corner to come face to face with a mother grizzly bear and her two cubs, I would become, I'm sure, instantly fearful. That's natural and unavoidable.

But Kodak wasn't walking alone in the woods. It was striding through the world, practically owning the whole idea of taking pictures. The company knew its industry—in fact, it practically invented photography itself—and knew its competitors. It knew the advantages of digital photography, which it had invented, after all.

Company executives knew as much as they could possibly know about the things they needed to do to transform Kodak from a giant in film photography into a company of similar dominance in digital photography.

The only thing they lacked was courage to do what everyone at the company realized needed to be done. Instead of taking that step, they decided to sit around and milk the Kodak cow of cash as long as it remained standing.

6

The Risk of Doing Something New

I am often amazed at the number of people who acknowledge the presence of risk in business but try to avoid it in practice. You can't be foolhardy with your career, your vocation, your business or your family's future. But you can't pretend that risk is like rain, either—something you can escape beneath an umbrella or a roof.

Here's my take on the subject: The more you avoid risk, the less likely it is that you'll achieve all that is possible within your own capabilities. Risk in business, as in life, cannot be avoided. But it can be managed.

We all manage risk dozens of times a day, on different levels. Each time we cross a busy street we risk being struck by a passing vehicle. We manage the risk by waiting for a break in the traffic before stepping off the curb. I may make similar risk management decisions dozens of times each day without thinking about the process.

> " The more you avoid risk, the less likely it is that you'll achieve all that is possible within your own capabilities. "

So you can't avoid risk. But it's not risk that caused the collapse of Kodak, or limits the achievement level of people. It's a special kind of fear: *the fear of doing something for the first time.*

Even when we have prepared ourselves in every way possible, our first attempt at achieving a goal is inhibited by our never having done it before. This is easy to understand when it involves an activity whose risk is easy to grasp, such as downhill skiing. We all deal with our fears at various levels and usually find a way to conquer them. But when we encounter fear in our careers, we may deal with the feeling not by conquering it but by deciding to avoid the situation that created the fear—even if the situation represents an opportunity to achieve a new level of success.

This attitude is as common among top managers and entrepreneurs as it is with any group. Wherever a fearful situation occurs, if it is not acknowledged and dealt with, the result will be the same: paralysis among even very competent people, and failure either to take advantage of opportunities or to deal with pressing issues. And it's a difficult thing for many people at all levels of business to recognize in themselves, but I have witnessed it over and over, in my business and in those of competitors and associates.

Most ambitious business people know their job involves finding new and better ways of doing things, but often they secretly resist change. Why? Not because they fail to recognize its importance but because they fear that, in doing something for the first time, they won't do it as well as they'd like or as others would expect.

I dug into some research on this problem and discovered that even among the most driven executives and entrepreneurs, fear of trying something for the first time is rooted in at least one, and frequently all three, of the following:

Fear of being wrong. People at every level in an organization share this fear. Lower-level employees fear the wrath of senior executives, who may berate staff members for making any decision that does not lead to complete success. Top-level executives fear that a setback of any kind may taint their future career prospects. Sometimes it does, but there are enough exceptions to make me doubt that it's a certainty. Like Peter Munk.

In the late 1950s, Munk and a partner formed a stereo company they named Clairtone, and within a few years the two Canadians built it into a leader in home electronics. People such as Frank Sinatra and Hugh Hefner were promoting the company, raving about the futuristic designs of its stereo cabinets. Things went well until Clairtone moved into colour television at exactly the wrong time. Unable to meet the technology advances and pricing of companies like Sony and Toshiba, Clairtone sank out of sight by 1970. Having learned a lesson in electronics, Munk switched to gold mining, launching Barrick Gold in 1983. Barrick is now the largest gold mining company in the world and has made Munk one of the world's wealthiest men.

Okay, not every business executive can be Peter Munk. But neither should every business person who has a setback believe his or her career is over.

Doubts about the goal's significance. If the impact of success isn't substantial, no one will notice if you succeed, but everyone will know if you fail. Solution: Don't make any decision at all!

This happened once when I was speaking to a salesperson at

one of our branch offices. We were preparing to make a sales pitch to a company that I considered a major prospect, and I asked her how things were going in preparing the presentation.

"Fine," she said. "Everything's in place." Then she told me that when our senior programming engineer visited her office as planned in a few months' time, the two of them would set up another meeting to finalize the sale.

"Why are you waiting so long?" I asked. "Why not go for it now?"

She hesitated before saying, "I would just feel better if he [the engineer] was along with me."

I knew that the true source of her problem had nothing to do with the presentation she had prepared for the customer, or with the need for an engineer to help with programming or installation matters that might arise. It had everything to do with her underestimating the importance of the deal and probably her own ability to make it a success. She didn't need the engineer to go with her and make the sales pitch. Waiting for him to arrive meant she could put off the decision and delay what she feared could be an embarrassment to her if the sales pitch failed. Some people are so afraid of the word "no" that they do everything in their power to delay hearing it. I prefer to find out quickly if an opportunity is going to close or not than to spend weeks hoping for an opportunity that turns out not to be real. Hope is an emotion, not a strategy.

Fear of being socially isolated. This may be the least logical but the most prevalent fear of all where decision making is concerned. Failure is bad enough; being *branded* a failure by co-workers is even worse in the minds of most people. The obvious question is "Why should you care what other people think?" Yet most people will continue caring about the opinion of others more than they will care about their opinion of themselves.

One of the most difficult challenges to overcome as you move up the corporate ladder or build the business you created is dealing with the decisions you need to make. The bigger the stakes, the more often you need to make calls on subjects you have never dealt with before. At times like these, it's easy to focus more on the risk than on the achievement. Some people actually obsess about the risk to the point where they are unable to either measure or manage it, leading to the paralysis I spoke of earlier.

Worry and concern are normal when making major decisions, but obsessing about potential failure leads to self-doubt, performance anxiety and resistance to change. It also leads to negative attitudes that can infect an entire team.

Ten steps toward doing something the first time

Even high achievers encounter fear when making decisions that involve doing something for the first time. We all need a system to help us move past the paralysis that accompanies this kind of fear and make the decision needed. Here are the steps in my system:

1. Assess the alternatives. The biggest source of fear is the unknown, and this applies to every aspect of life. Remove as much of the unknown as you can and you'll eliminate an equal amount of the fear in making a decision. Look at all potential outcomes, both good and bad, and weigh both the risks of failure and the benefits of success.

2. Measure the cost of missed opportunities. Think of your career as a balanced investment portfolio. Every good financial advisor will confirm that an ideal portfolio includes both low-risk and somewhat-risky investments. It's the somewhat-risky portions that deliver the most upside gain; without them, your investments are not likely to produce maximum returns. You can't exploit opportunities without taking risks. And without exploiting opportunities you will never create something new, never move past mediocrity and never make your mark on the world.

3. Accept your status as a novice. It's natural to feel comfortable doing things you have done many times in the past and to feel vulnerable when confronting something you have never done before. Don't beat yourself up over it.

4. Build a support network. This can consist of as few as one person, as long as he or she shares your attitude as a high achiever. Ask that person to check on your progress and serve as a source of feedback whenever you encounter a challenge on the way to your goal.

5. Define the worst-case scenario. What is the worst that can happen if your decision doesn't lead to success? How long will it take you to recover? If your lack of success means a few months spent getting back on your feet, which is worse—this short detour or a life of mediocrity? When I started my first business, my wife, Diane, and I considered what would happen if it worked (lots of upsides) and what would happen if it didn't (we would have to survive on her salary while I looked for a job to pay the mort-gage). The upsides outweighed the downsides, so we went ahead.

6. Check the long-range view. Consider what will happen over the next five to 10 years if you do not act now. If you are truly driven to achieve the level of success you crave, you will not want to be in the same place as you are now. But you will if you fail to make an important decision now.

7. Look for a dividend from failure. If I am faced with a decision to hire one of two people and both have equal qualifications, one of the questions I might ask is, "Have you ever started your own business?" If one person always worked at a comfortable job in a large corporation, and the other has launched a business that failed, I will invariably choose the second candidate, because he or she has learned more from the pain of failure than the other would ever pick up during a comfortable career.

This point brings to mind the story of a couple of Italian brothers from San Francisco who had been doing well making hydraulic pumps and aircraft parts. When they developed a new treatment for arthritis in the early 1950s, they thought every-body would want their product and began marketing it widely. But sales were depressing, and the failure almost cost the brothers their company, until they realized that the appeal of their prod-uct was not health as much as luxury—people just enjoyed being pampered and feeling the relaxation their product delivered. So they learned from their failure, shifted their focus and made bil-lions. Their name: Jacuzzi.

8. Reduce the downside. It's about managing risk. Create a contingency plan that can enable you to retain as much of the status quo as possible. You don't always have to work without a safety net.

9. Remember: Second-guessing is for losers. Once you've gathered as much material as possible given the time frame, don't start moving in a circle looking for weaknesses you have yet to find. Some people call this playing devil's advocate. Forget about it; the devil has enough advocates. Stay on the side of the angels. In most cases, even a flawed plan is better than no plan at all.

10. Do it. Nothing reduces fear and builds confidence better than taking action, but take it only after giving the idea as much thought as you can afford. Then do whatever it takes to make it work. I go through loads of "What if?" scenarios before making a major business decision, but once the decision is made, I go full steam ahead without looking back. First make your decision with confidence. Then make it work.

7

Seeing the Rain in a Drop of Hope

If there is one word in the English language that is overused, it's the word "impossible."

Many things in my lifetime could not have seemed remotely possible until they happened. Like arriving in North America at the age of eight, unable to speak any English, and becoming a network television personality. And having barely 20 dollars between my parents and me when we landed, yet amassing the kind of wealth I currently enjoy, all of it directly earned—no inheritance, no lottery winnings—from my efforts.

Is it unusual? Yes, it is. But it is not impossible.

A switch in a windowless room

Saying the word "impossible" is like flicking a switch in a windowless room; as soon as it is spoken and believed, the lights turn off and everyone stumbles around in the dark.

Nothing is impossible to achieve by anyone with the drive and the capability to make it happen, and no one—*no one*—knows for certain if they have the capability until they test it.

Many years ago, just after graduating from university, I lacked the ability to think on a large scale, to picture creating a national or even a global corporation employing thousands of people and generating millions of dollars in revenue each week. It just wasn't in my blood, and I doubt if it's in the blood of most people. For most of us, our horizons when we are young are limited to our own needs, and only when these are satisfied do we widen them and permit ourselves to set seriously bigger goals.

> " Saying the word 'impossible' is like flicking a switch in a windowless room; as soon as it is spoken and believed, the lights turn off and everyone stumbles around in the dark. "

When I was interviewed for a magazine article some time ago, the writer asked what I would do differently if I had to do things over again. When I replied "Nothing," she said her story required me to come up with a solid suggestion. "Okay," I said. "I would have dreamed bigger."

It's true. When I was younger, I did not know people could start their own business, I did not know how people became TV stars, I did not believe I could finish a marathon with a body not made for running, and I did not believe people could own their own airplane. Since I did not know how these things were done, I could not understand how to make them happen. Had I known they could be done by me, I would have aimed to do them sooner. The lesson: Don't let the size of your dreams limit the scope of your capabilities.

Many of us, however, do enjoy one quality that others may not possess: an ability, once the first promise of success appears, to recognize how much further we can take that promise and broaden our horizons almost instantly. Or, as I put it when discussing this idea with a friend, "Show me a drop of hope and I can see the rain."

"Show me a drop of hope and I can see the rain."

A few years ago I was reflecting on all that I had managed to accomplish so far in my life, and instead of feeling immense pride in my achievements, I felt vaguely uncomfortable. I was lacking something in life, and I realized it was a new challenge, a new way of testing myself to see if I could succeed at something I had never tried before. I felt I had things to achieve, but I was unclear about what they should be.

I was no longer taking risks. I don't mean foolish risks like jumping off buildings with a parachute or skiing down mountaintops. I'm a risk taker, but I'm not foolhardy. I refused to take risks that began with me saying to myself, "I'll bet you can't do that!" All the risks I took were carefully calculated, weighing the upside against the downside, looking for the return.

Along with my approach to risk, I was dealing with something else at the time—something that occupied my attention far more than any roll of the dice ever could. My mother was suffering from the cancer that would ultimately claim her life. One way of battling the distress I felt was to set myself an entirely new goal, focus on it for an extended period and try to meet it. Achieving the goal would be less important than diverting my mind from what the doctors told me was inevitable. She was diagnosed with stage 4 ovarian cancer, which meant there was little or no hope that she would survive.

My mother was in hospital for almost a year, and all of us knew there was little chance of her leaving alive. I visited her almost every night, remaining at her bedside sometimes until two in the morning, returning home with both my head and my heart filled with despair. As the only child of immigrant parents, I had relied on both of them to guide me through the challenge of fitting into a new society that was in no hurry to accept me. We had remained close, and the prospect of my mother no longer being there for me, even long after I had established myself in business and with my own family, was devastating. The greatest asset I enjoyed while growing up was my mother's love and support. She was my greatest cheerleader. Now, as a parent myself, I suspect we often try to do too many things for our kids when what they need most is simply someone to believe in them.

One day, on the way home from the hospital, feeling totally drained and beyond tired, I realized I couldn't continue at the pace I was going. Instead of assuming I needed more rest, I told myself that I needed to find a way to do more. So to deal with the anguish over my mother's condition (even if just for an hour a day), I began running. I discovered I was able to banish all the pain and sadness I was feeling about my mother's illness when I ran, and I was soon running an hour or so every day. When I ran, I didn't see anything else. Running is not easy for me, but I have always believed that if you are hard on yourself, the world will seem easier on you. Running became my friend, my companion and my escape from depression.

Sometimes timing and fortune come together in surprising ways. As my mother's condition grew worse, I could not bear to visit her every day. Seeing her in that state had become difficult for me, and she often never knew I was there anyway. One day when I was skiing with my family at our chalet, I told Diane that I needed to visit my mother and I wanted to leave immediately.

"You just saw her," Diane said, meaning I had visited my mom a couple of days earlier. "Why do you want to go now?"

I told her that I didn't know, that I just had to leave, and I did. I drove straight back to Toronto and her hospital room. She was heavily sedated, as she had been for most of my recent visits. I sat by her bed and took her hand—and in an incredible moment of clarity she opened her eyes. I saw no pain in them. They were the same beautiful eyes I had always known. She smiled at me and said "*Volim te*"—I love you. Then she smiled again and she was gone.

I can control and I am responsible for most things in my life, but I believe that a much greater force guided me to my mother's side on that particular day.

With my mother gone, other concerns arose. The deep recession of 2008–09 was in full swing. Companies were failing everywhere, and the effects were being felt at the Herjavec Group. The hour or so that I set aside to run each day became vital to me, but it was more of a duty than a challenge. I needed both a symbol and a fable, a sense that by succeeding at one thing I could inspire success at something else. Maybe, I thought, if I could try something that was at least improbable and maybe even impossible, and succeed anyway, the economy would improve and my business would survive. That was my fable. That is what I needed to believe. But what would the symbol be? I found it when I woke up one morning in the middle of December. I would enter the Miami Marathon at the end of January, a month and a half away.

I have always kept myself in good health and decent physical shape, but I was not blessed with a runner's physique. In Croatia, where I was born, the most valued physique in a man involved big strong bones and plenty of muscle to move them. The only endurance that mattered was the stamina to work in the fields from sun-up to sundown, day after day. Being able to run at 15 kilometres an hour for nearly three hours may have been a good trick in a Croatian rural village, but it didn't get the crops off the fields nearly as well as a strong back.

So running was never easy for me, which may be why I enjoy it so much. Each time I run is a test, and each test I complete successfully is its own reward.

> **Each time I run is a test, and each test I complete successfully is its own reward.**

Running fascinated me for various reasons, including the fact that the challenge involves strictly you, your body and your determination. That's all. You have no other team members to share the load and no sophisticated equipment to give you an advantage over others. You don't need expensive skis and boots, or a bicycle built with space-age equipment and computerized gimmicks. You don't have a faster car, or a bigger, more advanced tennis racquet than others. All you have is your legs, your lungs and your willpower. Your uniform consists of shoes, shorts and a top. There are no excuses if you fail. There is only you to blame.

The more I looked into competitive running, the more I realized it was against my nature. I'm a hyper guy in a high-tech business. My entire career has been based on speed and growth, and running against the clock and other runners in a marathon would involve pacing myself. Marathon running is not about speed alone. If I were interested in getting from point A to point B as fast as possible, I wouldn't be running. I would be driving one of my Lamborghinis or Ferraris. Once I began training for the marathon, I realized the lesson I was learning: Running was teaching me how to fix on a long-term goal and make it to the finish.

Running at my own pace and for as long as I chose wasn't difficult. But running a marathon would be a serious challenge. I had never attempted to run 42 kilometres (26.2 miles) before, and training to run a marathon that was just six weeks away would be . . . well, some people might suggest it was impossible, which was enough for me to insist on doing it.

I was confident about my ability to reach any goal that I set for myself. For once in my life, I may have been too confident. Instead of seeking experienced coaching to prepare myself for the race, I set my own training schedule. Big mistake. Somewhere, for example, I read that marathon runners should eat lots of carbs before a race. So the night before the Miami Marathon, I visited an Italian restaurant and wolfed down its spicy Italian sausage and pasta bowl. Hey, I was ready!

The next morning, standing there among 18,000 other marathoners, I heard the starter speak over the public address system just before he fired the gun to begin the race. "Runners," he told us, "just remember that this is the last 26.2 miles you have to run." That was inspiring. It gave us a goal that we could keep in sight. Then the gun sounded and I was off.

Running a marathon is a motivating event for many people, especially a run for charity. Waiting for the starter's gun, you see signs all around you announcing those who are running in memory of a loved one or in support of a worthy cause. Standing there in Miami, remembering my mother, I was ready to go.

The beginning was fun. I was inspired and motivated, up near the front with the fast runners. But the beginning of a race is always fun. At mile 6, I was running so well that I began planning to qualify for the Boston Marathon. I was on fire, running faster than I had ever run before, telling myself that if I could rack up a good time in Miami, I could run with the best in Boston.

Or maybe not. Around mile 11, I lost the spicy Italian sausage and pasta bowl. At mile 16, I started to believe not only that I would not finish the race but that I might not even survive it. I believed it right up until I saw the man running ahead of me deal with an even bigger problem than mine: his metal leg fell off. Along with some other runners, I stopped to help him replace it, then resumed the run, realizing that I had nothing to complain about. All I had to do was suck it up and finish the damn thing.

I did finish, barely. I spent the next two days in bed, overcoming the effects of doing something I had not been prepared to do, but succeeding anyway. One way or another, the impossible was now reachable.

When the agony of my first marathon faded, my determination returned. I had overcome one "impossibility." Why not another one? Why not the New York Marathon? This time I trained properly, and when the starter's gun sounded on that day in early November, I was in the best shape of my life. I ran the first 10 miles or so with total confidence at a blistering pace for me. Once again I was on fire . . . for a while. Then my calves began to freeze up. For the last 10 miles or so it was almost impossible to run, and I wanted to sit down, watch the rest of the runners go by and ease the pain. And I would have, except there were so many well-wishers along the way that I could not get off the route. Finally I asked myself out loud, "Are you a loser?" When I didn't respond to my own question, I kept repeating it over and over, talking to myself aloud, almost shouting, "Are you a loser? Are you?"

This is a trigger I use on myself. I don't like to fail and I refuse to be considered a loser by anyone, especially myself.

I kept asking myself if I was a loser, until I heard my wife call from the curb as I passed her, "Go, Robert—you can do it!" Amazed that Diane had found me in a crowd of 50,000 runners, and inspired by her words, I finished the race. Best shape of my life, six months' training at a high level compared with no training for the Miami Marathon—and I finished at a slower time! Not with the time I had hoped for, but with the knowledge that I had not given in to the urge to sit on the sidelines and watch others do what I had intended to do. When you're tackling the impossible, you take inspiration from wherever it appears.

Anybody who says something is impossible risks being interrupted by someone doing it

Each of us can achieve far more than we imagine, but only if we persuade ourselves that "impossible" isn't a fact, it's an opinion. I remember hearing someone explain Terry Fox's achievement. "Imagine running a marathon," he said to the person who wasn't aware of all that Terry Fox had achieved. "Now imagine running a marathon every day, seven days a week, with no days off, for almost five months. Pretty difficult? Now imagine doing it with only one good leg."

It sounds impossible, but it really happened.

None of us is free of dreams, but most of us give them up because we believe they are impossible. We take a half-hearted run at making our dreams come true and, at the first barrier we encounter, decide that whatever we have done is "good enough."

If we do this, we will never know what was truly best.

8

Bare-Knuckle Lessons

I don't believe you can build an active and agile mind inside an unfit, out-of-shape body. Mental and physical condition are linked in most people. This doesn't mean becoming a marathon runner will lift your IQ to genius levels, or that people whose physical disabilities prevent them from working out suffer mentally as well. Far from it. But your ambition to be successful should always include time to pay as much attention to your body as you pay to your career.

You gain many side benefits from physical conditioning. Running, working out or even taking long, brisk walks releases your mind to deal with problems that may appear unsolvable. A phrase from ancient Roman times sums it up best: *Mens sana in corpore sano*—A sound mind in a sound body.

I'm as fascinated by people who achieve greatness through their physical abilities as I am by those who become powerhouses in business. In many ways, it's a matter of applying the same kind of thinking to achieve different goals. Whether you want to become

the leader in your business field or stand
on the podium at the Olympic Games, the
route to success follows a similar course
through the three Ds: determination, dedication and drive.

**"The route to success
follows a similar course
through the three Ds:
determination, dedication
and drive."**

I have been fortunate to meet a number
of my personal heroes and discuss their
approaches to achieving success. They all told me variations on the
three Ds theory, but some had more pointed ways of explaining it
than others.

Launching a career by facing down a bully

Georges St-Pierre is one of the most interesting people I have
met, and he gave me some unexpected advice. If you're a fan
of mixed martial arts (MMA), you don't need to be told who
Georges St-Pierre is or what he has accomplished in his career.
His life is a morality lesson with a fairy-tale plot line, except that
it's all true.

Georges was seven years old when a school bully decided to target him for abuse, stealing his clothes and money. Georges reacted
by insisting that his father teach him karate, and he absorbed the
lessons well. Thanks to Georges's skill at karate and his determination not to be bullied, his tormentor was taught a lesson and
Georges grew as tough mentally as he did physically.

Georges had found his calling, soon moving beyond his father's coaching abilities to study with a Kyokushin karate master. As
a teenager, he added wrestling, boxing and Brazilian jiu-jitsu to

his training regimen, for a time paying for his lessons by working as a garbage collector.

Georges is not a big man. He stands about 5 feet 10 inches tall and weighs about 170 pounds, which qualifies him as a welterweight in Ultimate Fighting Championship (UFC) competition. Of 24 UFC matches, Georges won 22, most by a TKO. The intensity of UFC matches, with almost no holds barred, is unmatched in any other sport, and much of the competition is based on intimidation. You are inside a cage with another person whose strategy for winning is to overpower you to the point of killing you, if he chooses to. All of this happens in front of 50,000 or more screaming fans. It's the closest you can come to a street brawl, which may explain why it has become one of the world's fastest-growing sports.

Guess what Georges St-Pierre fears most?

Georges still retains the French-Canadian accent he acquired while growing up in Saint-Isidore, Quebec, and of course, he is in amazing physical condition. A guy like Georges can intimidate you even when he's being his own laid-back self, so I was curious to know if he was ever afraid when he walked into the ring for a UFC match.

I love his response.

"Robert," he said, "I am never afraid of what another human being can do to me. I am only afraid of causing myself shame. Of disappointing myself. That is my greatest fear. In the ring, it is my only fear."

People who are not in sports don't understand power

I also wanted to compare the way Georges and I work out. I run a good deal because of my interest in marathons. More than anything else, I want endurance, the ability to keep pressing on toward my goal, whether it's the end of the marathon or some complex business deal I'm working on. I assumed that Georges, like me, would do a lot of cardio training.

Georges surprised me. He wasn't interested in that kind of endurance, he told me. He was interested in a special kind of power. According to Georges, people outside professional sports misunderstand power. "Power," he said, "is efficiency. It is not necessarily strength or endurance."

> " Power is efficiency. It is not necessarily strength or endurance. "

Georges and other UFC fighters need enough strength to last just five rounds, but more than anything else, they need to draw upon sudden strength at key moments. A lag in response, or a muscle suddenly going tired or flabby, can lead to disaster. UFC fighters need training to develop "fast-twitch" muscles, powerful responses from the body that occur almost before they realize they're needed. You don't develop that kind of conditioning in the usual manner, such as lifting weights to build biceps and triceps. In Georges's sport, too much muscle can be disastrous. Anyone with a body even close to the kind displayed by champion weightlifters, or body-building competitors with sculpted muscles, wouldn't finish the first round in a UFC match.

(Georges's body, by the way, is "cut," as bodybuilders call it, to show off his muscles in dramatic fashion. He agreed that this doesn't help him win bouts. When I asked why he bothered then to shape his body that way, he smiled and said, "It makes me look good to the women.")

Georges doesn't need shear strength. He needs efficiency and response, along with the mental toughness associated with championship athletes.

When I met Georges he was with Henry Martinez, a buddy who outweighed him by as much as 100 pounds. "So, Georges," I said, "could you beat Henry here in a UFC bout?"

Without a moment's hesitation, Georges nodded and said, "Henry, he's a strong man, for sure. Stronger than me. But I don't train for strength. I train for efficiency."

Georges and I had a great talk. For a guy who makes his living finding ways to hurt people to the point where their lives are literally in his hands, he's very friendly. I liked him. And his comments on strength and power gave me a good deal to think about. The idea that enough power of any kind will solve all your needs and ensure that you achieve all your goals is nonsense. Dinosaurs were the largest, most powerful creatures to ever walk the earth, but you don't see too many of them hanging around downtown these days, nor stomping through the jungle for that matter.

In business, we have seen many powerhouse companies fade away for various reasons. Some of them lacked endurance. Others were simply inefficient, or lost a killer instinct. It was because he had that instinct, Georges told me without any sense of bragging, that his only fear was the fear of shaming himself with a poor performance.

When I arrived in Canada, the most prominent name I heard in business was "Eaton's." A whole generation has grown up not knowing that Eaton's was a retailing behemoth. Eaton's had a department store in the downtown core of every city and a catalogue in every home. It had its own private brands, its own traditions and, until the 1950s, its own slogan: "The largest retail organization in the British Empire." Retailers from the United States visited Canada to study Eaton's retail methods for themselves. It was as impossible to imagine Canada without Eaton's as it would be to imagine the country without snow in the winter.

Today, there is not a single Eaton's department store left. The company sank out of sight in 1999. Why? Because it had everything going for it except those fast-twitch muscles, the kind that helped Georges St-Pierre win MMA titles year after year. Without fast-twitch muscles and the courage and determination to use them, the store was unable to respond to a changing world around it, one that focused on suburban malls rather than midtown locations and emphasized low pricing over often stuffy service.

> " If you lack the response of fast-twitch muscles, the ability to turn on the power as soon as it's needed instead of mulling over the situation while the opportunity fades, you're handicapping yourself. "

If you have the endurance to reject mediocrity and reach the highest goals you set for yourself, congratulations. And if you develop enough strength for yourself, your team and your organization to exert the power to get things done, you have achieved a good deal.

But if, along with these qualities, you lack the response of fast-twitch muscles, the ability to turn on the power as soon as it's needed instead of mulling over the situation while the opportunity fades, you're handicapping yourself.

And that's what I learned from my friend Georges St-Pierre.

9

Nobody Deserves Anything

I love many things about Canada.

I love the way it welcomed my parents and me, two adults and a child with little more than a dream between them, and gave us the opportunity to make that dream a reality. I love the way it opens doors to people who want to climb as far up the ladder as their talents allow, yet does not forget those with needs on the lower levels of society. I love the fact that I arrived here with nothing, yet the prime minister presented me with the Diamond Jubilee Medal for my contribution to Canada. And I love the fact that we can all disagree about the things that constitute Canada without, for the most part, losing our respect for those on the other side of the argument.

Mind you, the transition from the kid with the funny clothes and the thick Croatian accent to the guy in a Tom Ford suit who appears on network television all across North America was not always a walk in the park. Canada may have welcomed me, but I recall some bullies in public school who weren't nearly as hospitable. My experience probably wasn't much different from that of other immigrant children who arrived at the same time as me, or of those who landed in Canada at other times in the country's history. Most of us not only survived various challenges but also grew more determined than ever to prove that, yes, we did belong here, and we were going to make a positive difference with our presence.

In my case, those experiences made me who I am, in many ways. Because of that immigrant experience, that sense of being an outsider, I expect that I will never lose my need to prove myself over and over. My wife, Diane, often asks me, even after nearly 20 years of marriage, "Why do you always want to do more? What makes you so motivated?" She believes I carry a big chip on my shoulder, and she may be right. I think most people who have something to prove to the world feel the same way, challenging the world one way or another.

Why the attitude? Much of the answer can be found back in the playgrounds and on the streets where the bullies hung out after school. They left that chip on my shoulder, and it will never go away, no matter how much I achieve and how famous I become. I cannot forget what it felt like to be the weird-looking dumpy kid who got beat up or insulted at school. The experience created a complex mix of emotions, including insecurity and fear, and the need to keep proving myself over and over again.

It also instilled in me a belief that neither I nor anyone else deserves anything except the right to prove ourselves. I did not "deserve" my success, nor did any of the people who work for me and with me.

Nobody gets what he or she "deserves" from life, because the truth is, we deserve nothing. No one owes any of us a thing; we each get from life what we make of it. The only person responsible for your success or failure is the person you look at in the mirror every morning. It's true that some of us have a head start. But the most driven of us can begin far back in the pack and still win.

> "Neither I nor anyone else deserves anything except the right to prove ourselves."

Success starts with sacrifice

Some people, when learning of my background, have asked me why so many immigrants are successful at business. What enables someone who lands in a foreign country to achieve levels of success that others, whose Canadian ancestors go back several generations, cannot seem to attain?

The answer is sacrifice. Immigrants who achieve great success in business are willing to sacrifice today's security and comfort for tomorrow's achievements. I know my father didn't enjoy walking an hour each way to work every day just to save 50 cents in bus fare. And he certainly would have craved a job more meaningful and satisfying than sweeping a factory floor all day long. But it never occurred to him that he deserved more. In fact, I don't think he believed that he deserved anything in life he didn't earn.

I don't believe that Darwin's "survival of the fittest" theory applies to individuals where their work is concerned, or that we exist in a do-or-die world where we eat only what we kill. There is too much of life to enjoy, and too much satisfaction to be earned from our efforts, for me to draw that kind of parallel. (I think it should apply to corporations, however—if a company cannot compete, it must make way for others that can.) I love the fact that so much encouragement and so many resources are available to anyone starting a business in Canada, compared with most other countries.

When I speak to college and university students across North America, I remind them that they are living in a time when they can begin learning about becoming an entrepreneur while still in school, instead of suffering the hard knocks of doing it all on their own. That's an amazing head start, and they should take every advantage of it.

The things that I have achieved in my life give me pride, but I don't stand around patting myself on the back. That's a useless, self-centred response. Besides, none of my achievements was entirely a solo act. They were scored thanks to both a team effort and my own guiding principles. For example, I've never pretended to be the smartest guy in my company. I have probably been the most driven, however—a guy willing to stay up all night if necessary to get the job done. And a substantial amount of credit for my company's success must go to a policy I have maintained when choosing new employees: I hire people who are smarter than me.

I also take the legal concept of a corporation as a separate entity literally. My business exists, in my mind, as a living, breathing being, and I am responsible for its care and growth. It needs attention, it needs feeding, it needs guidance and sometimes, yes, it needs discipline. It may survive without my direct and daily attention, but it won't grow and mature unless I am there, in some form, to provide the necessities of life, and if that sounds simplistic or even childish, I don't care. The imagery works.

The importance I place on ensuring a corporation's constant growth and maturity, similar to a parent's concern for a child, relates directly back to not settling for "good enough." Businesses are sustained from two sources of energy: good management and clear vision. The first is self-explanatory. The second is part of being an entrepreneur.

Many people assume that an entrepreneurial spirit represents the launch pad for new businesses, and once the business is established, the entrepreneur must transform himself or herself into an effective manager. This may happen in some instances, but when it does—when someone with entrepreneurial skills attempts to morph into a full-fledged manager—the seeds for the demise of the business, I suspect, begin to sprout.

The mindset of an entrepreneur is obviously essential to launch a business, but on its own it lacks the skills needed to maintaining a business. The day you abandon the mentality that was the impetus to start a business is the day you should turn it over to someone else to manage. Years of earning a tidy profit may have you believing you deserve your success and can relax, letting the business run itself. When you begin believing that, you are set-tling for "good enough." And when you settle for "good enough," you are handicapping yourself and everyone who depends upon you for their own successful career.

Before you create wealth, you must create value

Some people who are aware of the wealth I have created through my working life find it difficult to believe that a similar chance to achieve success is available to them. But it is. We may all be unique individuals, but opportunity is universal. Unfortunately, too many people focus on the idea of creating wealth exclusively, and that's the wrong route to follow.

Before you can create wealth, you have to create value, a fact that's not on the radar of many people who arrive at *Shark Tank* looking for investment capital. Creating sufficient value in your business—*real* value as opposed to the value that exists only in your dreams—translates into wealth eventually. The more value you create, the more wealth you accrue.

The difference between earnings and value, when viewed in this context, may become so obvious that it shouldn't need explaining. But it does. If you create a company with measureable value and want only to take money out of it, go look for a buyer, not an investor.

10

Mediocrity Is a Virus

Attitudes are contagious. Every military officer knows this, and every business leader should acknowledge it. When I speak to salespeople at the Herjavec Group about a prospective new client or an exciting new product or an aggressive new sales strategy, the salespeople give me back the same energy I feed them. And if, after scanning a sales presentation, I were to announce it was "good enough," I could expect a disappointing effort and a less than successful result. Nothing is ever "good enough"; it is either excellent or inferior.

If I were to promote an idea that I could not fully support or I couldn't feel totally confident in its success, my lack of enthusiasm would affect everyone, but the effect would be most noticeable on the highest performers in the team, the ones who are motivated to do their best in every situation. It's a fact: winners not only want to associate with winners, they want to be *inspired* by

> " Winners not only want to associate with winners, they want to be *inspired* by them. "

them. How much inspiration can you get from a leader who is too easily satisfied?

The greatest satisfaction I have ever enjoyed in my business is the satisfaction earned by setting the highest standards of which I am capable, persuading others around me to set similar standards and watching it pay off with surprising levels of success. I never have and never will shrug at a subpar effort and say, "That's probably good enough."

And I will never believe that I deserve anything of value that comes my way without working for it.

Neither should you.

Six steps to business success

I see things from the point of view of a businessman, but many lessons I have learned over the years apply to anyone with ambition. The six steps listed below are good examples, and they apply at any level in an organization.

1. Build and maintain networks. The old saying that it's who you know more than what you know is partly correct. If you don't know anyone who can assist you to reach your goals, get out and meet them. Use your ambition to succeed as a tool to overcome your shyness. And here's the payoff: if you succeed sufficiently, you will become somebody who others will want to know.

Start building inner networks consisting of relationships with key peers, advisors and mentors. Depend on them not for leads to new business but for support and direction when you need them. Dedicate time to providing the same benefits to them when called upon. There are few places for successful lone wolves in any business.

2. Keep yourself customer-centred. The best way to ensure that your mind and energy are fixed on the success of your business is to focus on the needs of your customers. Whether you are a top executive or an ambitious underling, only when you fully understand your customers' world and appreciate their needs will you be equipped to make decisions that will ultimately benefit your business and your career. The purpose of every business, after all, is to create customers.

3. Practice humble honesty. When things are going well, you're convinced that you can succeed at anything. When things are going badly, you begin to believe that nothing you do is effective. Neither opinion is good. You need to honestly assess your strengths and weaknesses, because no matter how much you have achieved and how much more you expect to accomplish, you are not perfect in every area.

4. Work on your strengths. Once you have identified your weaknesses, don't waste precious time trying to eliminate or improve them. Use that time to apply your strengths, and find someone who is strong in the skills that you lack. Research has proven that successful people focus on their strengths and delegate others to perform tasks in areas where they are weak.

5. Remember that Murphy is always just down the hall. Things never go as you planned them. No matter how carefully you examine a situation and anticipate problems, Murphy's

Law will apply somewhere, sometime. The only way to deal with this certainty is to remain adaptable. Teach yourself to respond to unexpected surprises and unforeseen events by changing course and taking action, even when you don't have all the information you would like.

6. Know an opportunity when you see one. The business world is filled with stories of otherwise bright people who passed up opportunities that changed the world and could have changed their lives. Like the business executive who believed xerography was a dumb idea, or the publishers who rejected J.K. Rowling's manuscript for the first Harry Potter book. These are extreme examples, but opportunities arise for businesses every day. Be alert to the presence of real opportunities, and respond quickly to those with promise.

How do you do that? Here's a hint and an example.

During World War II, pilots flying at night had to be aware of approaching enemy aircraft and respond to it. Without radar, they depended on their night vision to spot other planes, which meant watching for the glow of the other aircraft's exhaust or in some cases its flying lights. They soon learned that it was easier to find a weak light in the inky blackness of the night sky not by looking directly at it, but by being aware of it in the periphery of their vision. In this way, they were more likely to spot a threat.

Use the same approach in business and you may be more likely to spot an opportunity. It worked for me when I began to realize the growing importance of the Internet—along with almost everyone else, of course. In the 1990s, it became obvious that as the Internet expanded it would be carrying confidential data and, ultimately, large volumes of money in some form or another.

The direct view was to find ways of jumping on the bandwagon, looking for ways to move the data and the money around. Good idea, I thought. Then I got a better idea by looking at the prospect from an indirect angle—from the periphery, like the fighter pilots at night.

Whether moving secrets or money, Internet users would soon become fixated on doing it out of the grasp of unauthorized people. What the Internet really needed, I realized, was not another means of moving the data around but a means of doing it safely and securely.

The Internet created an opportunity for people who could use it in a profitable manner. And their use of the Net created an opportunity for me to help them do it safely. So while almost everyone else was jumping on the bandwagon, I created companies to help the wagon keep rolling safely.

11

How to Kick Your Own Ass

I'll admit it: some mornings I wake up believing that I face more problems than solutions, and that I will encounter more failures than accomplishments. When this happens I have to find a way to boot myself forward. Or, to add some colour to the idea, I need to kick my own ass.*

I have various ways to do this, including exercise. Running eight kilometres is difficult. Running 12 kilometres is even harder. If I run 12 kilometres when I feel like running only eight, I raise my level of determination and, while my problems may not shrink in number, my confidence in solving them balloons in size.

The technique has worked for several years, but I am discovering that the larger my business grows, the more difficult

---

* My *Shark Tank* colleague Mark Cuban has a different take on this. His words—"Every day somebody somewhere wakes up with the sole purpose of kicking your ass"—impressed me so much that I had them engraved on a plaque to display in my office.

it is to find that necessary motivation. Why? Because I have so much less to lose if things go off the track.

Urgency is a great motivator

Early in my career, the loss of my business would have meant the loss of everything that my wife, Diane, and I had worked to achieve. As the business grew and our lives became more secure, it was easy to become lazy compared with how we were in the past. I explain it this way: Someone running from a burning building made of wood has a very clear sense of motivation. The same person in a stable structure made of concrete won't feel the same kind of urgency. Urgency is a great motivator.

That's what kicking your own ass is all about—being able to summon up the motivation to get going even when the need doesn't appear urgent. Rick Hansen has it. Oxford University didn't have it, and may still lack it. I never attended Oxford, but I have met Rick Hansen. Both of them teach a lesson worth learning, though each comes from a different direction.

> " Urgency is a great motivator. That's what kicking your own ass is all about—being able to summon up the motivation to get going even when the need doesn't appear urgent. "

The risk of lacking motivation

In November 2000, a shocking event occurred at Oxford. A professor named John Kay, who had been appointed head of Oxford's business school, resigned just three years into a five-year contract. His resignation, he announced, was based on his concern that Oxford was about to become a mediocre institution, more interested in coasting on its 1,000-year-old tradition than in reaching new levels of excellence.

Oxford, Professor Kay warned, risked becoming a second-rate educational institution unless it overhauled its bureaucratic structure and learned to compete with the modern world. The school had to cut back on something Kay called "fudging and compromise." It needed to make critical decisions more expeditiously, adopt a more aggressive stance where policies and procedures were concerned, and "rid itself of its morass of committees with ill-defined and overlapping responsibilities."*

In response to Kay's charges, someone at the upper levels of the university declared, "There is no doubt that Oxford remains a pre-eminent world class university. We continue to attract top-level academics and students from all corners of the world." The message was clear: Oxford saw no need to change its approach to dreadful things like budgeting, decision making and accountability.

All of this was, as various outlets of the British media put it, something of a tempest in a teapot back in 2000. In that year, depending on your source, Oxford was rated among either the top three or the top. five universities in the world. Five years later, it had slipped to tenth place in the Academic

---

* This and the next two quotations are from Caroline Davies, "Oxford University 'risks slipping into mediocrity,'" *The Telegraph*, November 20, 2000.

Ranking of World Universities, the most highly regarded system of listing colleges and universities according to their excellence.*

Being rated tenth best university in the world is something to brag about, assuming the people at Oxford really care about such standings. But slipping from top spot to tenth while claiming that the university saw no need to change the way it was managed might have alerted the people at the top that the school risked sliding even further down the ladder. If so, they have not revealed any plans to change.

Oxford has not asked me for my advice, and I don't expect it to ever do so. If it did, I would bypass all the intellectual analysis and management jargon and simply suggest the university, as an entity, learn to kick its own ass.

That's not the usual kind of proposal heard in the halls of Oxford, I'll bet, but maybe that's part of the problem. Too often, organizations avoid taking necessary and sometimes painful steps by sending the problem to committees, where, if all goes well, it will be talked to death. It's understandable. We all have to force ourselves to do things we would prefer not to. Sometimes it takes a kick in the butt from our boss, our spouse, our friends, our physician or someone else to persuade us that things must change. But these people are not always around to do it. And few of them know as many of the details, the risks

---

* Universities are rated according to academic or research performance (including Nobel Prizes and other awards won by alumni and staff), highly cited researchers, papers indexed in major citation indices, and per capita academic performance.

and the benefits as we know ourselves. That's when we need to kick our own ass.

Just to take the analogy one step further, being kicked in the butt may hurt, but it tends to push us forward, and forward is the direction we need to go if we're sincere about moving beyond problems and reaching our goals. Just ask Rick Hansen.

Things you can do that you don't know you can do

I met Rick and his wife during a charity event and, frankly, I was a little nervous at first.

We all measure our achievements in different ways and subconsciously compare ours with others'. Meeting someone who launched a business and reached a level of success comparable to my own is something I always look forward to; we can quickly understand the obstacles the other faced, and the means of overcoming them.

> " We all measure our achievements in different ways. "

But Rick Hansen's achievements are almost impossible for the rest of us to even comprehend.

Just to remind everyone: At age 15, Rick was an all-star athlete in his hometown of Williams Lake, British Columbia. Baseball, hockey, football, track and field, you name it—Rick performed better than anyone else in his school and community. He was also bright and good-looking, and it was clear that any path he chose, especially one associated with sports, would be available to him.

Then, one day in 1972, he and a buddy went fishing. On the way home they decided to hitchhike, and when a pickup pulled to the side of the road, both boys jumped in the back of the truck, unaware that the driver was drunk. When the vehicle veered off the road and hit a tree, the two boys were vaulted out of the bed of the truck. Rick's friend walked away with nothing more than a few bruises. Rick's spine was shattered. He would never walk again.

"For the first five years," Rick told me, "I would have given anything, I would have given my soul, to have the use of my legs back." Then he smiled and said, "Now, I wouldn't change a thing." I believed him.

Nobody feels sorry for Rick Hansen anymore. Besides a wife and family, he has the admiration and support of millions of people around the world.

In his early 20s, Rick grew inspired by the Marathon of Hope that Terry Fox had been determined to complete, running across Canada on one leg as a means of raising funds for cancer research. By this time Rick was a stellar wheelchair athlete and the first student with a physical disability to graduate with a degree in physical education from the University of British Columbia. He eventually won three gold medals, two silvers and a bronze at the 1980 and 1984 Summer Paralympics.

Rick decided to emulate Terry Fox in his own way. He obviously couldn't duplicate Terry's efforts to run across Canada. Instead, he would propel his wheelchair around the world, counting on the strengths and techniques he had perfected while winning 19 international wheelchair marathons, including three world championships. Money raised during his Man in Motion World Tour would be used to fund research on the treatment of spinal cord injuries. Over 26 months, beginning in March 1985, he propelled his wheelchair 40,000 kilometres through 34 countries on four continents. Like Terry Fox, he struck a responsive chord everywhere he went. More than a million people greeted him with cheers when he entered Beijing, and by the time he returned to British Columbia in May 1987, he had raised more than $26 million for his cause. Since then, his efforts on behalf of helping people with similar injuries have raised another $175 million.

After meeting Rick, I walked away feeling a little like an underachiever, saying to myself, "Wow—I've gotta get to work. I've gotta do something with my life!" That's the kind of impact he makes on people.

It's ironic that I'm using Rick Hansen, whose legs have not moved of their own accord for almost 40 years, as an example of kicking your own ass. He is, however, a perfect illustration of what can be accomplished not because of our abilities but in spite of our disabilities.

Too bad Oxford University doesn't have the same attitude.

Six ingredients needed to reach success through excellence

1. Purpose. Many people have difficulty identifying this quality, but it exists nevertheless. Having a purpose in life is the reason you get out of bed in the morning, and achieving your purpose makes you happy—or should. Whatever your purpose, it has to be worth the sacrifice you'll make in time and energy. Think of Rick Hansen facing every day knowing he had to propel his wheelchair 40 or 50 kilometres forward, using only the strength of his arms and his grip on the wheels, before nightfall. His purpose made it worth the effort.

2. Endurance. The surest way to achieve your purpose is to aim for excellence in every aspect of your work. Committing to excellence is a good news/bad news situation. The good news: You can start right away. The bad news: You'll never finish.

3. Courage. When others declare that something is "good enough," it takes courage to disagree. And when others are either bored with a project or convinced that the goal can't be reached—and you know in your heart that it can—you need to be brave enough to keep going. You also need nerve to become visible when necessary—to step out of the safety of your comfort zone into the limelight and be prepared to accept kudos if you win and possibly derision if you fail. Successful leaders do this very well. I'm not sure that the administrators at Oxford were as successful.

4. Optimism. Believing that the best is yet to come and that all of your goals are reachable is more than an attitude. It's an asset as important to your success as any skill. It's also good for your health. I would never give up my physical exercises, but I'm convinced that none of the cardiovascular workouts I perform is more beneficial to my health than the optimism I draw upon day after day.

5. Passion. No one believes in the importance of passion in every aspect of life and business more than I do. I look for it in every employee I hire and in every business pitch made to me. It doesn't have to be flamboyant, and it definitely can't be phony. It has to be sincere, and it must be grounded in reality.

6. Joy. Spreading joy attracts people toward you. Being miserable drives people away.

12

The Law of 24

Everyone has his or her own explanation for success or failure in life. Especially failure. Except with failure you don't actually get explanations. You get excuses.

Ask 10 successful people to explain how they managed to win in an arena where so many others have lost and you'll get the usual reasons. Hard work. Preparation. A great team. A good product. Plus large quantities of passion, energy and organization. The list is valid, but the contents are like the ingredients of some spectacular dish provided by a bunch of chefs. You may know the ingredients, but you don't know how much of each you'll need and how to mix them properly. It can be more confusing than enlightening.

When it comes to determining the most important ingredient of success, we need something that is easy to remember, unquestionable in its logic and applicable to everybody in every situation. In my mind, the best source of advice has been, of all people, Woody Allen. "Eighty percent of success," Woody said, "is showing up." It may not be his funniest line—not as funny as "I'm not sure if there's an afterlife, but I plan on taking a change of underwear just in case"—but it's true. Many people dream of success, and I assume they show up in their own dreams. Too many just happen to be absent in their own reality.

Michael Jordan had his own way of making the same point. "Some people want it to happen, some people wish it would happen, others make it happen." When I quoted this to someone once, they replied, "And some people stand around and ask 'What the hell just happened?'"

The same number of hours in everyone's day

We all want to do better in our lives. It's the human condition. Without a need for personal achievement and improving the amount of comfort and security we enjoy, mankind would be back living in caves and wearing bearskin suits. Even when an acceptable level of comfort and security has been reached, for most people there are still rungs to climb. It's just that the ladders reach to different places. Some people want to find universal truths, others want to express themselves in music or writing and still others set up their ladder to reach goals in politics or other endeavours.

Whether your ladder is set up to climb to self-fulfilment or enormous wealth, you may find yourself lagging behind others who seem to reach the top rung of every ladder they scale, while you're still on the lower rungs. How did they do it? What makes the difference between those who reach the top and those who are left near the ground?

Many people want to know the difference because they believe it will help explain why they failed to achieve the level of success they have been seeking. Were successful people just plain lucky? Did they go to the right schools, meet the right people, make friends in high places? Were they ruthless and greedy, or just cold and calculating? People stuck on the lower rungs of their career ladder tend to lack many of these measures, so there is logic to their reasoning.

But consider this: instead of listing all the differences between successful and unsuccessful people, think of the one thing common to all of them—in fact, common to everybody on earth. *They all have the same 24 hours in a day to get things done.*

Like Woody Allen's explanation of success, this may seem overly simplistic. We all know there are 24 hours in a day. What's the big secret in that? The secret isn't in their existence or our awareness of it. The secret is in what we do with the same amount of time that is handed to everybody each day. It's those same 24 hours.

Instead of using them to measure time, visualize those 24 hours as dollars. Imagine that each day, every day of the year, you are handed 24 dollars to do with as you please. How will you spend them? You could gamble the money on lottery tickets, horse races, slot machines or some other potential method of getting rich quick. You could spend it on alcohol or drugs for their momentary pleasure and worry about the consequences later. You could borrow against your 24-dollars-a-day and take a luxury vacation, paying off your two-week holiday with the next 50 weeks of income. Or you could treat every dollar as though it were something prepared to work for you—which is the way to treat every hour in every day that you wake up healthy and active.

All the successful people I know show up each day and work hard, and not one of them resents it. In fact, their attitude is just the opposite: *they love it.* They love looking back on the same 24 hours granted to all of us each day and measuring what they accomplished. If you can do the same thing—achieve more in the same amount of time than others around you, and know that you are moving toward some goal that you have set for yourself—you are or will be successful.

And here's the rub: the less you have, the more you need to do with the time that's given you. People with greater means can leverage more resources; people with lesser means can't, so they need to do more on their own with every minute available to them.

Too many people waste the hours given them the same way they might waste money handed them. They waste it in four ways: by procrastinating, by losing focus on important things, by thinking too much and doing too little, and by lowering their eyes to look at the downside instead of lifting their heads to see the upside.

People procrastinate because the job at hand intimidates them. Ask procrastinators to sharpen a pencil and they'll hop to it. Ask for a project that stretches their knowledge to its limit, and they'll spend time doing other things. Like sharpening pencils. The best cure for procrastination is to break the task down into smaller elements and do one element at a time. Instead of feeling overwhelmed when faced with writing a report covering, say, a dozen aspects of a marketing plan, think of each aspect as a short chapter in a book. Writing an entire book is daunting to most people; writing a single chapter sounds more doable. Later, you can link the "chapters" together.

Losing focus on important things happens to people who don't understand the Pareto Principle. It is like the law of gravity: everybody can understand what it does, but nobody is sure how it works.* Essentially, it means that 80 percent of the effects come from 20 percent of the causes. Marketers and economists know all about the Pareto Principle. It confirms phenomena such as:

> " The Pareto Principle essentially means that 80 percent of the effects come from 20 percent of the causes. "

- 80 percent of beer is consumed by 20 percent of drinkers
- 80 percent of income is earned by 20 percent of workers
- 80 percent of sales come from 20 percent of products
- 80 percent of health care costs are spent on 20 percent of the population
- 80 percent of crime is caused by 20 percent of criminals

It sounds frivolous, but the principle keeps getting proven. A recent United Nations Development Programme report, for example, showed the richest 20 percent of the world's population control 82.7 percent of the world's income. Applying this

---

* The Pareto Principle is named for the Italian economist Vilfredo Pareto, who, in 1906, noted that 80 percent of the land in Italy was owned by 20 percent of the people. He developed the principle after finding that 80 percent of the peas he harvested from his garden came from 20 percent of the pods. He later connected the ratio to almost everything else in life.

principle, then, would mean that 80 percent of results stem from just 20 percent of activities. And I'll bet you know what those 20 percent represent. Using the Pareto Principle, you can identify the 20 percent of the things you do that generate 80 percent of your reward, focus your efforts on the 20 percent and reap the returns.

Thinking too much leads to paralysis by analysis. It's important to think things through, but many people use thinking as a means of avoiding action. Thinking, they may submit, enables them to achieve something while awaiting the perfect time to take action. But there is no such thing as a perfect time to do something. And if there is, it's gone almost before it arrives. Whatever needs to be done should be done *now*.

There's a downside to everything (including life itself). Get over it. Finding faults and weaknesses is the most efficient way I know of killing new ideas and personal motivation. Make the decision, move forward and watch for problems as they arise—then deal with them one by one. I love the quote from designer Giorgio Armani, who said: "You think you've made it and yet the next day's press will always be waiting for you, the public will always ask more of you. In short, you can always do better!"*

---

* CNN International.com, Q&A: Giorgio Armani, October 3, 2006, http://edition.cnn.com/2006/TRAVEL/06/01/milan.qa/.

Goals, visions and elephants for dinner

The best way I know to keep motivated through the hours allotted to us each day is by setting goals that are worth attaining. Being goal-oriented is hardly new advice, perhaps, but don't assume it's as simple as walking from point A to point B on a sunny afternoon. It's almost never a straight line. Reaching a worthwhile goal involves curves, hills, detours, switchbacks and the odd dead end. The secret is to keep moving forward and build momentum. How? By finding ways to keep focused on the target and maintain your enthusiasm. Here are seven:

1. Make your goal exciting. Passion is at the core of everyone who won't settle for less than finishing first. Choose a goal that taps into the passion that drives you to succeed in the first place. But passion is just the price of admission. People on *Shark Tank* often say, "You should invest in me because I am passionate about what I do." Passion alone means nothing. It's a given that you are passionate about succeeding because otherwise you wouldn't be standing in front of us Sharks looking for money. Passion is fine, but it's like believing you can win a marathon because you have two legs. You need much, much more.

2. Set a schedule. Without a time frame, a goal is just a wish. Some people link their dreams to the word "someday," as in "Someday I'll open my own office," or "Someday I'll finish my degree," or even "Someday I'll write a book." "Someday" isn't a real day like Monday or Tuesday; it's just another word for "never."

3. Keep your goals realistic. We're encouraged to dream big dreams, but don't confuse dreams with reality. Picture your goal as a target, and you want to hit the bull's eye. Now it's a matter of being realistic. If you're too close to the target, hitting the bull's eye won't mean much to anyone, including yourself. If you're a mile away, you're likely to be always off target. Set a goal that's both within reach and satisfying. Believing you can move mountains is fine, but first you need to learn how mountains are moved. Ambition without some degree of skill or knowledge achieves nothing. Every successful entrepreneur I have met has been an expert in one key area: creativity or communications or accounting, you name it. Identify your expertise, then make the most of it.

4. Assign at least one of those 24 allotted hours each day to achieving goals. We all encounter day-to-day urgencies that can't be avoided. Somewhere in the day, you need to apply time-reaching goals you've set for yourself. Dealing with urgencies exclusively is like walking on a treadmill; something gets done but nothing goes anywhere. Find time to get off the treadmill and make progress. It's like thinking in the eye of a hurricane—a means of stepping away from the chaos surrounding you now and then. Each of us can do this in a different way. Find yours. Whether it involves reading a book, working out or taking a walk, discover it and use it to help maintain your sanity in an often insane world.

5. Make yourself accountable. All the promises you make to yourself will be worthless if you find it easy to ignore them whenever you please . . . or if you "can't find the time." The best way to avoid this is by making yourself accountable to others—your co-workers, spouse, partner, family, friends or anyone with whom you are comfortable sharing your goals and aspirations. Draw on them for strength, courage and consultation when you need it.

6. Reach the goal in your mind before achieving it in your life. This technique has been called "psycho-cybernetics," and it's all about imagining how to reach your goal before attempting it. It's not a new concept, but it is as effective as ever. Back in the 1950s, psychologists discovered that athletes who mentally pictured successfully competing in their sport scored more victories than those who didn't.* Pole vaulters and high jumpers would imagine every step they took to reach the bar and rise above it; tennis players would picture their ideal serves and returns; football receivers would imagine running perfect patterns on specific plays and catching the ball every time. In almost every instance, picturing the achievement in the mind yielded improved results in reality. The idea is to eliminate negative feedback, and it's as applicable in business as anywhere.

7. Remember the only way to eat an elephant—one bite at a time.

---

* Maxwell Maltz, who originated the concept, proved its effectiveness with an experiment on three basketball teams. One team practised an extra hour each day for a week on the basketball court, making free throws. The second team didn't practise at all. The third team spent an hour each day sitting on the court while mentally practising making free throws. After a week, the team that had practised making free throws on the court outscored the team that didn't practise. And the team that had practised mentally performed as well as the team that had actually practised.

13

A Secret Source for Great Employees

One January day, I booked a meeting room at an exclusive private club to review prospects for the coming year with the sales staff. It was to start as a luncheon meeting and extend through most of the afternoon. About 20 people would be attending, and I left it to the club management, who is good at organizing these meetings, to set up the tables and ensure everything went off smoothly.

The first member of my sales staff to arrive was a young woman named Dakota, who walked into the room, surveyed the set-up and immediately announced to the manager, "This won't do." She pointed out that the tables were crowded together, the sightlines were not good, the pathway to the front of the room, where the presentations would be made, could be improved for better flow and the lighting was too bright.

Overriding the manager's protests, Dakota took action, politely instructing him to move the buffet table out of the meeting room and into the hall. This made space to reposition the tables. Recruiting assistance from a bystander—an outside consultant who was attending the meeting—she moved the tables and chairs, adjusted the lighting, and relocated the projector and projection screen, all before anyone else arrived.

When I got there, the room set-up looked ideal and the sales meeting went well. It was only later that the consultant recalled Dakota's quiet, take-charge attitude.

What happened would not be a big deal if Dakota had been our meeting planner or a senior staff member with years of experience in arranging and attending these meetings. She was neither. She was a 19-year-old member of our internal sales staff, barely a year out of high school.

The consultant who witnessed Dakota's authoritative approach was amazed, especially when he discovered that no one had instructed her to ensure that the room was properly set up for the meeting. She just happened to be the first to arrive and chose not to wait for others to do the job.

When I heard how Dakota had handled the situation, I was pleased but not surprised. I was especially happy that she was not concerned about setting up the room "the way Robert likes it" but simply recognized that things were not ideal and immediately took charge to correct them. She was reflecting the culture at our company. Reviewing and assessing situations before taking the action necessary to optimize things is part of the culture that we work within.

Fly-halfs, point guards and clear thinking

I also knew where and how Dakota drew on her decision-making abilities, because she was chosen for exactly those qualities. Dakota is a member of Canada's Under-18 National Women's Rugby Team, which defeated the USA to win an international tournament. Her position on the team is fly-half, which I understand is similar to the point guard position in basketball, her other sport. Point guard, Dakota explained to me, is a decision-making position, and playing fly-half in rugby also involves making decisions. Which is one of the reasons she was hired directly out of high school to work at the Herjavec Group.

I'm not that familiar with rugby, so I looked up "fly-half" and learned: "Good fly-halfs are calm, clear-thinking and have the vision to direct effective attacking plays. Fly-halfs need good passing and kicking skills. Often the fly-half is the best kicker in the team and needs to be able to execute attacking kicks such as up-and-unders, grubbers and chip kicks as well as being able to kick for territory."*

I didn't look up up-and-unders, grubbers and chip kicks; the description of fly-half told me enough.

As much as any other skill that a potential new employee may bring to the company, serious involvement in competitive sports is something I look for. As soon as I hear that someone has played on a championship team or proved themselves winners individually over a period of time, I know I'm dealing with

---

* Tony Biscombe and Peter Drewett, *Rugby: Steps to Success*, 2nd ed. (Human Kinetics, 2009), 148–49.

a prospective employee who is goal-oriented, self-disciplined and determined to win. They may need someone to show them how to do something the first time, but once they understand their role, they rarely need anyone to tell them what to do and when to do it.

Both of our daughters are competitive swimmers, participating at both the provincial and national levels. Swimming requires enormous amounts of time to prepare for a few seconds of competition, which means you need to have total commitment to the sport. On a typical weekday I'm up at 4:15 a.m. and rouse my daughters by 5:00, so they can swim for two hours before leaving for school.

> "As soon as I hear that someone has played on a championship team . . . I know I'm dealing with a prospective employee who is goal-oriented, self-disciplined and determined to win."

They may participate in the Olympics someday, but I'm more interested in knowing they enjoy the competition and even the training. I also know that they are absorbing an important life lesson as well. They are learning that nothing worthwhile is achieved without sacrifice. "One day you will go out into the real world and people will complain to you about how hard they work," I have said to them. "They will tell you how early they have to get up each morning and how little time they have for other things. And you will not really understand what they are talking about." Athletes grasp the importance of hard work and aiming for a goal. You don't have to teach them that. And that's why I like hiring athletes.

I'm not sure how many employees of the Herjavec Group participate in competitive sports. I know as I write this that the staff includes a young man who attended university on a golf scholarship, another who won a basketball scholarship and a sales representative who once was a serious contender for the title of fastest man in the world over 100 metres.

It's not just the rowers who move the boats

You don't have to be a gifted athlete in order to score high on the potential employment index. Many people participate at different levels in sports because they thrive on competition and want to put their leadership skills to good use.

Think of a coxswain on a rowing crew. The rowers tend to be large, muscular and trained to work as a smoothly operating team. The coxswain? Generally a smaller person, to save weight on the boat. Instead of physical strength, the coxswain brings other qualities to the team that are as essential to winning as the power applied to the oars. These include:

Knowing the team's state of mind. Spectators see the coxswain at work only when the rowing hull is moving along the water, with the coxswain in back, shouting the strokes and steering the boat. His or her role is just as important between races, when the best coxswains know how to either inspire or calm down the rowers as needed.

Dividing responsibilities according to needs. Championship rowers can have brilliant minds as well as muscular bodies, but during competition it's their physical abilities that count the most. This leaves the coxswain to apply his or her skills in leadership and direction.

Providing inspiration and pacing. Each rower knows only his or her measure of performance. A coxswain can and should survey the entire vessel, aware of what the team is capable of achieving and pushing it to do it.

For all of these reasons, I tend to favour employees who have experienced tough competition and who have met the challenge of preparing for it. Academic training alone can't provide all that's often required in the arena or stadium, or in a business environment. Competing at the highest level available teaches important skills and attitudes that purely academic studies can only hint at.

So, what's the downside to hiring sports competitors? Unless employees recognize that being competitive and goal-driven does not ensure that they will forever rise in the standings at the same pace, they may feel plateaued or dissatisfied at some point. If you're actively involved in competitive sports and have big ambitions for your business career, you have an advantage that is both apparent and valuable to your employer. Just remember to pace yourself. You probably want to shoot to the top of the league. That's understandable. But no ball player ever went from sandlot games to the World Series in one season, or even five.

14

Never Underestimate the Power of Fun

More than 100 years after Charles Dickens wrote *A Christmas Carol,* some employers are still being associated with sour-faced Ebenezer Scrooge. A few even see themselves in a similar role—not to the extent of forcing people to work on Christmas Day and refusing to show compassion, but by assuming that work is serious business that demands commitment and focus from every employee.

Here is my first response: Yes, work is serious business.

Here is my second response: But not all the time.

The Herjavec Group did not become one of the fastest-growing companies in its industry by treating the things it does lightly. It got that way by treating its work and the needs of its clients seriously. Very seriously. Which is why we try to inject as much fun into the work experience as possible, while still recognizing the responsibility we have to our clients.

Protecting clients with our version of a war room

I launched the Herjavec Group as a means of providing maximum available security to the Internet operations of our clients. In many ways, we are like a private police force hired to provide 24/7 protection by keeping out trespassers, intruders, burglars, con artists and plain old peeping Toms. It's a very different kind of business from the virus protection programs that you use for your home and business computers.

You provide protection for your personal computer, or you should, by installing software from companies such as McAfee, Symantec and Kaspersky, among others. Most of your concern is focused on viruses and malware that can slow or even cripple your computer, as well as access your personal information.

If you're concerned about a couple of home computers, just imagine having 10,000 or more, all susceptible to similar challenges. Then imagine that your computers are used to transfer millions of dollars back and forth *each second of the day.* The money moves on an electronic conveyor belt, past the eyes of criminals around the world who know where it is coming from and where it is going and will make every attempt possible to divert some of into their own hands.

That such criminals are out there may not surprise you, but the scope of the industry and the steps needed to provide protection to clients likely would. Our responsibility is substantial because the risk to our clients is huge. As a result, the pressure that we work under can be equally enormous, and the methods we use to deliver our service are complex.

Our clients include major banks and other financial institutions, along with a few government ministries. We assess their needs, then choose, modify and install software that best matches those needs. Our real service, however, is active. We don't just build the bank vault; we stand next to it and watch for suspicious characters lurking around.

We do this from a room that is as advanced in its own way as anything you might find at NASA. Only a handful of our staff is permitted inside. Each of them has been investigated and cleared by the RCMP, and entry is impossible until they pass both a palm-print and an iris scan. In the dimly lit room, they face a bank of flat-screen monitors feeding data on every client's network, looking specifically for attempts at unauthorized access. Whenever one is spotted, action is taken to block the attempt and identify the individual behind it. We also target new techniques being used to break through firewalls and other protection devices, and develop the means to prevent them from succeeding in the future.

It's all reminiscent of movies from the 1960s showing military personnel in a war room, tracking unidentified aircraft entering North American air space and dispatching jet fighters to intercept and, if necessary, shoot down the intruder. In fact, that's an ideal analogy: we are a private NORAD, watching over the borders of our clients' networks, armed to the teeth with the latest technology and prepared to blast the enemy.

> **"We are a private NORAD, watching over the borders of our clients' networks, armed to the teeth with the latest technology and prepared to blast the enemy."**

That's a little dramatic perhaps, but when you are protecting the assets of clients doing several billion dollars in business transactions, it's a serious responsibility. The serious side of our business also makes having fun a little more difficult and much more important. We do it through group activities, and the tone is usually set by me.

Trusting my senses

At the Herjavec Group, I trust my senses to tell me when it's time for employees to get together somewhere off-site just for the fun of it. We invariably return to our routine invigorated, with a greater sense of teamwork and accomplishment.

This practice can confuse some people who, because of their profession or position, don't fully understand it. One of them is my wife, Diane, a physician. "Why do you have so many of these events?" she asked me once. "Why do people have to combine work with recreation? Can't they keep them separate?"

"Yes, they can, but I don't want them to. I don't want employees coming to the office strictly to do a job," I said. "I expect them to show up because they want to be there more than anywhere else during their working day. And the best way to encourage this is by having fun from time to time."

It's normal, I suppose, for skeptics to question which is cause and which is effect when evaluating the benefits of having fun at work. Do happy people produce successful companies, or do successful people seek companies offering an appealing work environment? It's a classic chicken or egg situation, and my answer is: It doesn't matter. The only thing that matters is the correlation between employees liking their job and companies performing at above-average levels.

However, some guidance is needed in choosing employees who are likely to respond to an atmosphere of fun with enthusiasm, productivity and loyalty. Here are three qualities that, along with other qualifications, could help determine the best candidates:

Team spirit. Emphasizing team spirit is a direct reflection of my appreciation for competitive athletes and their dedication to winning. People who engage in softball tournaments, bowling leagues, golf weekends and other fun sports activities will be the members of your company with maximum team spirit and, almost certainly, above-average performance.

Small-town outlook. This isn't a hard and fast rule, but many employers give points to candidates from small towns over those from large, sophisticated cities. Why? Because, so the theory goes, small-town folks are more careful about the way they treat people. You can't avoid a bad reputation in a village as easily as you can in a metropolitan area. If you lose your reputation for honesty and fairness in a big city, you can always find people to whom you're a blank sheet of paper with no black marks next to your name. In a small town, your reputation is accessible to almost everyone, thus you're more careful about how you deal with people.

Life plans. People who think ahead in both short-term and long-term measures are more committed to their careers and their success than those whose vision rarely extends beyond the next paycheque. They're also more likely to respond to being part of the organization both when the pressure is on and when it's time to relax and have fun.

Ten ways to measure productive fun

There is a serious side to having fun, or there should be. Any event that generates conflict or resentment will be worse than unproductive; it could lead to tension, silo mentalities and unnecessary employee turnover. Here are 10 ways to judge if an event fits the bill:

1. It makes people smile. Better yet, it generates laughter.

2. It reminds people of their value to the company, to the team and to each other.

3. With the possible exception of annual commemorative events, it is inexpensive to launch, easy to set up and requires limited time and space. It's not important—or even necessary—to spend a lot of money on an event. It's only important to encourage people to have fun.

4. Its emphasis is on feeling good about one another and the organization. Every effort must be made to avoid embarrassing or offending anyone both inside and beyond the company.

5. It is inclusive, while respecting the right of members to opt out without feeling peer pressure or being subjected to ridicule. As your company grows you need to change the kinds of events it offers. As a small company, we would schedule paintball fights, which were lots of fun for 10 hyper-competitive guys. When we grew larger, with a wide cross-section of staff, I had to accept that not everyone enjoys getting blasted with a paintball gun and having welts on their arms and legs.

6. It does not detract from anyone's ability to perform his or her job safely, professionally and efficiently.

7. Ideally, it reflects and supports the company's culture and core values, and certainly never contradicts them.

8. Its occurrence is timely: it should be frequent enough to maintain the desired level of enthusiasm but not so frequent that it loses its spontaneity and uniqueness, or interferes with achieving corporate objectives. Find the balance.

9. As much as possible, it is planned and implemented by employees; avoid the paternalistic atmosphere that can be created when activities become the exclusive responsibility of management.

10. Its results are identifiable and measureable.

15

Large Frogs Need Big Lily Pads

Lately, my company has been doing a good deal of business with IBM. I'm especially familiar with this firm because my first years in the computer business were spent marketing and promoting one of its products.

I had never entered the company's national offices, however, until I met with the president of IBM Canada. He had set up a meeting to discuss our future plans and how our companies could gain advantage by working together. A large data storage company the Herjavec Group had recently purchased utilized several IBM products and services.

The first thing I noticed upon entering the IBM lobby was a plaque on the wall displaying a quotation from Thomas Watson, IBM's founder and a man acknowledged as one of the most brilliant business minds of the 20th century:

> *We are here to build a great company. We are*
> *here to build a company that will last through the*

ages. We are here to build a company that will last longer than you and me.

Two points about that quotation.

First, in an era when too many CEOs and their boards avoid looking beyond the next quarterly financial statement, these words serve to remind them that great companies are built on far horizons.

Second, Thomas Watson wrote those words in 1916, two years after he had been hired and a year after being named president. They aren't recent thoughts; they are almost 100 years old. IBM is making certain they are never forgotten by its employees.

" **Great companies are built on far horizons.** "

It took a lot of courage for Watson to stand in front of his employees, his customers and the rest of the world and vow to build a company for the ages. Only an individual with valour and foresight could dare make a statement so audacious and ensure that it became reality. Thomas Watson served at the helm of IBM for 40 years after saying those words, and many of his business concepts, including perhaps the most concise piece of advice of all time—*Think!*—remain valid today. His words inspired me as much as any business wisdom I have ever received, despite having been uttered almost 50 years before I was born. Among other things, they strengthened my determination to continue scaling up my company.

It's not just a matter of growing bigger—it's also a matter of growing wider

One of the most difficult things about business for many people to understand is the concept of scaling—finding ways to expand a successful firm into areas that enable it to grow not only higher but also wider, and do it in a methodical manner that benefits everyone, including employees and customers.

Scaling up a company effectively involves more than generating bigger sales and recording larger profits. Your company may grow higher that way, but it also needs to grow wider as a means of creating stability and fostering future growth, and this involves spreading the base of your products and services into new but related areas. To become a bigger frog you first need to find a bigger lily pad.

Steve Jobs, for example, scaled Apple in a limited but enormously successful manner, moving the company from personal computers to the iPod (connecting the company directly with the music industry), iPad and iPhone. All three product categories were logical extensions of **"To become a bigger frog you first need to find a bigger lily pad."** Apple's established success with its revamped iMac computers, and they built a wider base for the firm. Perhaps the biggest challenge to Jobs's successors will be finding new ways to continue scaling Apple. When you're the largest capitalized company in the world, it's often difficult to find a bigger lily pad, let alone a bigger pond.

Dell Computers, once a primary competitor of Apple, doesn't need a bigger pond. While it grew spectacularly well during the 1990s to match the growth of PCs generally, its scaling, compared with Apple's, was limited. As I write this, there are no Dell smartphones, no Dell products associated with the music business and no Dell products that extend beyond basic laptop or desktop computer operations. Dell based its early success on low pricing rather than innovation, which proves the point about successful scaling. If pricing is your sole, exclusive selling point, how do you widen your base when you are relying on others to introduce products that you can undercut with price? Dell has attempted to make this shift, with various levels of success, but moving from a marketing position based on low pricing to an image based on new product sectors is difficult. Will Dell succeed? We'll see.

Back to Thomas Watson. Notice that he said nothing about profits or dividends. He spoke only of growth and longevity. These are always the focus of successful scaling in business. Watson was intent on building a company that would outlast him and add value to the lives of future generations, and that's exactly what he did. As a lesson, it's almost 100 years old, but I believe it is just as significant today as it was when he wrote those words. Maybe even more so.

Scaling up by moving from security to total integration

I am always searching for new and appropriate ways to scale my company upward, looking for a larger and more solid lily pad.

The Herjavec Group made a major move when it acquired a firm engaged in data storage, a logical extension of the company's services to protect the integrity of its clients' networks.

Why storage? Because the need for storing data securely is growing at an incredible rate. The world is becoming based on access to data, and the volume of data accessed and collected is mind-boggling. In 2010, the chairman of Google claimed his company created as much data in two days as all of humanity had produced from the dawn of history to 2003.* With that much data being accessed, the opportunities are massive for companies that can move it, secure it, store it and integrate it efficiently. We are shaping the company into an integrator dedicated to solving complex business problems associated with IT services. The concept is powered by the recognition that today's businesses need global computational abilities that are open to authorized users and essentially seamless in their operations.

This is more difficult to achieve than you may think. Software programs have immense processing capabilities, but within many companies they are like islands in a very large lake— or frog pond, if you will. Hopping from one to the other and landing exactly where you need to be takes a good deal of navigation and knowledge. That's the service we at the Herjavec Group will be using to continue scaling up the company as an integrator, widening its base and elevating sales levels.

---

* Pamela Jones Harbour, "Why Google Has Too Much Power Over Your Private Life," *The New York Times*, December 19, 2012.

It will represent another step toward my goal of shaping the company into a mini IBM. Every step along the way, I'll be remembering Thomas Watson's words about building a company that will last through the ages.

16

The Biggest Challenge to Growth

My company has many competitors, and I respect them all, even though I may wish to obliterate some and buy out others. Competition makes us all better and, assuming we're winning more than we're losing—and we usually are—it makes the whole process fun.

By the way, I bear no ill will toward any of my competitors at any level. But business is a contact sport in many ways, and head-to-head competition is a zero-sum game. For us to win, someone has to lose, and for us to grow, we have to win many more competitions than we lose. If our success leads to a competitor's failure, it's unfortunate, but I don't regret it and I certainly won't apologize. That's my attitude toward my competitors, and I assume it's also their attitude toward me.

A few years ago, as my company continued to grow, I recognized an amazing fact:

> **"The biggest challenge to maintaining the growth and reaching our targets was no longer our competitors. It was our employees, both current and future."**

the biggest challenge to maintaining the growth and reaching our targets was no longer our competitors. It was our employees, both current and future. Don't get me wrong: the employees at the Herjavec Group are first-rate, as capable and dedicated as any in the business. The challenge is in managing, motivating and, as time passes, replacing them.

Dealing with ambitious people

From time to time I receive offers to purchase my company. I reject them all, but there are some days I begin to take them seriously, days when the idea is somewhat attractive to me. Those are the days when I'm dealing with complicated people issues.

I can handle the complexity of the business, the challenges of the products and the vendors supplying them, and I enjoy meeting customers. Even losing a big deal or taking on a tough competitor doesn't get me down. It energizes me. It's in my nature to face challenges head on, determined to win. It's the human issues that drain me and leave me staring out the window, wondering if I should hand the company over to someone else.

I built my company with the assistance of gifted, highly motivated staff with whom I maintained a personal relationship. We worked elbow to elbow, sharing high-fives when we scored a victory and gritting our teeth when we didn't reach our goal. The larger the company became, the less often we shared these moments closely.

I work to inspire my staff to aim for whatever goal they want to achieve within the company. I also present myself as the personification of the firm. My personal brand and the brand of my company are logically interlinked, and we all benefit from it. But the benefits come with complications, and the complications are usually the result of people issues.

The majority of the problems I encounter are related to employee expectations and access—expectations of reward for their work, and access to the guy to whom they feel loyalty. The expectations are high, and they are usually met. Some members of our sales staff have increased their income by a factor of 10 within just a few years of joining the Herjavec Group. I'm as proud as they are of their achievements. The problem occurs when they grow convinced that the graph line should continue moving steeply upward to infinity, taking their income with it. That's an unrealistic position, leading to their belief that they are underpaid, and creating enormous frustration.

I share their frustration from a different direction. While they delivered the goods to justify their impressive income— impressive even to me—I provided the environment for them to attain this success. I taught and encouraged these people to set and achieve these goals, so I shouldn't be surprised at their expectations, and they shouldn't be frustrated by my position. But I often am, and they sometimes are.

Most habits are bad habits—eventually

One of the key lessons in management I have absorbed over the years is that, while some basic management rules are universal— open communication, honesty and goal-setting, for example—

many other techniques have to be adjusted according to the situation. Having a team of long-term and productive employees is a wonderful asset to any organization, but longevity creates habits, and sometimes habits need to be broken.

Among the requirements of my role as a manager is having the ability to see in advance the need for change, determine how and when it will be made, and then motivate my employees to join me in making it. This is important in any business. Whatever skills or products or services brought you to where you are today will not necessarily carry you through the future. Every business leader needs to acknowledge this fact and act on it. In our industry, where small revolutions in technology can happen literally overnight, it's essential. Our people know this as well as I do. But, as I said, habits are difficult to change. People need more than a logical reason to break habits. They need a powerful incentive.

This was driven home to me recently when the Herjavec Group acquired a company that had been drifting for some time because of management problems. The employees knew of the problems, but without effective management they were unable to solve them. Our purchase of the firm generated a wave of relief and enthusiasm on the employees' part. One of them said our arrival "was as though the clouds parted and the sun began shining again." We brought new money for investment, new ideas to restart the operations and new direction that promised to make their jobs more rewarding and more secure. In this case, the employees didn't need any motivation to do things differently. They needed only new guidance, and we provided it.

When I said, in effect, "For years you have all been going in this direction, but starting today I want you to go in *that* direction," the response was, "How fast?"

Reality meets philosophy

Around the same time, I recognized that a few adjustments were needed to some of the procedures at the Herjavec Group. And here's where I had a revelation, an epiphany in understanding the challenge of management.

Our past success proved to be the biggest obstacle the company faced in achieving the growth levels we had set for ourselves.

This may sound illogical, I know. Success is supposed to breed success. The momentum of growth is supposed to help propel you forward to the next level of achievement, and then the one beyond that and so on. That's the philosophical intent, but reality has a habit of intruding on philosophy, and in our case that's exactly what happened.

All of our major sales staff have been with us for at least four years. During those years we have set sales records not only for ourselves but for our entire industry sector, and we have received every award available in our industry to prove it. More than that, our top sales producers have the commissions and bonuses to confirm it.

But that roller-coaster ride recently began slowing to a crawl at the top of the hill, and I didn't want to see what was waiting beyond the crest. We had finished the year at $65 million in sales, which represented spectacular growth over our previous year's level of $38 million, but I realized that we were getting complacent. The momentum was slowing, and it is much harder to restart stalled momentum than it is to keep it going. We had to change things. More precisely, we had to change direction. So, as I had done with the newly acquired company, I said, "Instead of going this way, I want you to start going *that* way." The results, however, were starkly different this time. The response was, "You know, I've been going this way for four years, and it's pretty good. Maybe I'll go in that new direction and maybe I won't."

No sales staff were ever disrespectful to me. No one seriously challenged the necessity or the wisdom of moving in the new direction if we were committed to reaching our targets. But that was on the outside. On the inside, the information was being heard, but it wasn't registering. While many staff were agreeing with my comments, they were saying to themselves, "Change? Yeah, I guess the company needs to change. But not necessarily me. And not necessarily right away."

That's what ingrained success can do to some people. It can swing their enthusiasm and their talents in different ways, and it is management's responsibility to see that success indeed breeds success and not inertia.

> " It is management's responsibility to see that success indeed breeds success and not inertia. "

You see it in sports all the time. A football team, a basketball team, a hockey team goes roaring through the schedule, winning game after game until it appears unbeatable. Then the same team loses to another that it should have beaten easily. What happened? It could be arrogance, overconfidence or a lack of focus on the better team's part, mixed with the determination and even the anger of the lesser team. Whatever the combination, it produces a loss for the team that should have won easily, and whenever this occurs, my first thought is, *"The coaches didn't do their job."*

The responsibility of coaches is not only to build and train a team capable of defeating its opponents. It includes making sure the team focuses on its goals and maintains a correct attitude, reminding a winning team how good its opponents are, and motivating a losing team to draw on its pride and ability to defeat Goliath.

In our case, we learned that not everyone wants to make the necessary change in direction. Not everyone recognizes the importance of rising out of a chair that has grown comfortable over the years and getting back on the track. It's like a regiment of soldiers that, after fighting a long and protracted battle, is told by its commander, "We have to get up tomorrow and do it all over again." It's difficult for both the soldiers and the commander. Sometimes the soldiers can't handle the thought of going back into battle. Sometimes they want only to rest. They are neither lazy nor cowardly. They just can't make the journey anymore. When this occurs, despite management's best efforts to make the necessary changes, drastic action needs to be taken. The expression often used is "bring in fresh blood."

In many ways, the only thing as difficult as moving old staff out of their jobs is choosing new people to replace them. Employees who have been with you for several years, regardless of their weaknesses on the job, are a known resource. Prospective employees, regardless of their education and job history, are an unknown potential.

One of the main questions I ask people who apply for key positions with us is "Have you ever worked for a small company?"

We want people whose work experience is rooted in companies with annual sales of $100 million or less, which, in the technology industry, is not considered large by any means. Large companies can teach you a great deal, but one thing they are unable to teach is the ability to focus on the future—on where the company is going rather than where it is coming from. Many of us in the Herjavec Group recall when we were excited about scoring $10 million in annual sales, and how elated we were to hit our target of $100 million. Our challenge is to recover that same emotional high as we aim for new targets, and newly hired employees from small companies are able to draw from that well of enthusiasm more easily.

One of the things I love about running a business like ours is the direct way we measure success. We made a huge number of changes that year, and it was tough on everyone. But they worked: our annual sales jumped from $73 million to $125 million. There is no better measure of success than watching the sales curve start climbing off the chart. This growth spurt was more than satisfying on its own; it qualified our company as one of the fastest corporations in Canada to reach $100-plus million in sales.

Slicing through the layers

As a company grows to 40, 50 and then 100 and more employees, it is essential to build multiple management layers. New staff won't find this a problem, but people who trace their employment back to the beginning may find it difficult to adjust.

It grows more challenging when managers effective at supervising a handful of staff are not equally effective when they have a dozen or more employees to handle. The problem occurs when the size of a business outgrows the maturity of its management, and this can lead to uncomfortable situations. Next to firing long-term employees, I don't know of anything more uncomfortable than informing managers who have assisted in building a firm's success that they need to relinquish their duties to those with sharper management skills—especially when the new members have been brought in from outside the company. In addition to losing the authority they once enjoyed, long-term employees now have to deal with a layer between themselves and their old buddy the business owner. This can create its own challenge, especially since I'm interested in being in the middle of the action wherever possible.

It's hard to make these kinds of changes. My natural inclination is to want people to like me. Unfortunately, this is an almost impossible expectation in a fast-growing company. I aim for "like," but I will take "respect." If the people around me respect my dedication and fairness, that's fine with me. I accept that, in the process of making an omelette, a few eggs are going to be cracked.

When the need to think overrides the need to act

I have never believed that any job in my company is too small for me to tackle if it needs to be done *now!* If the toilets need cleaning and I've got a brush in my hand, I'll tackle 'em. And if some sales calls aren't working out well, I'll tag along with the salesperson on the next visit to the client—which sometimes freaks out people at the client's. Like it or not, when faced with a problem I'm inclined to invest my energy in taking action.

If this sounds like a positive attribute . . . well, I'm not sure it is.

This propensity to act worked wonderfully when the Herjavec Group was little more than a start-up, and it helped the company grow over the next few years. The more time I spent acting on problems, however, the less time I had to think about them. And the bigger a company gets, the more top management needs to spend on thought rather than action. The amount of action a company of $5 million needs is substantial. The amount of action a company worth $125 million needs is insurmountable for an individual. This means adding layers of people to execute the ideas formulated by the CEO.

This often becomes a stumbling block to any CEO who happens to be the entrepreneur who launched the company, as in my case. I like to execute on a personal level. In the beginning, I was the guy who did the hiring, handled the salary negotiations, announced the objectives, delivered the bonuses and fired the people who weren't working out. Today I'm no longer the guy who does everything. Now I'm the guy who makes sure everything is done.

When a manager at my company tells an employee, "You have to improve this aspect of your work," the inner response is generally, "Yeah, I guess I better get around to that." When I say the same words to the same employee in the same tone, they carry a dose of drama with them. If I am dissatisfied with an employee's performance, the person knows that I am empowered to do something about it immediately. Without discussion. And probably without appeal.

If the business doesn't survive, nobody survives

Many of the difficult moments I have with personnel involve salespeople who, based on their success, were assigned management duties or believed they were entitled to a management role. Here's the Herjavec law of sales management (I didn't invent it, but I think I'm the first to hang my name on it):

Being an outstanding salesperson does not, on its own, qualify anyone to be considered an outstanding sales manager.

I'm sure there are exceptions to this rule, but I haven't found one yet.

You cannot begin a business with little more than a vision and a small group of people who share that vision and not become personally linked with those people. I say with all honesty that I love the people who first joined me in creating my business. The relationship extends far beyond work. I'm the godfather to some of their children, and in some cases we have shared both the joy and the gloom of work for more than 20 years. They effectively hitched their wagon to my dream, and together we made it a corporate reality. They became partners in both the dream and the corporation. But are they a permanent part of that dream?

Delivering bad news to employees is both difficult and essential, and the only way to do it is by knowing that the decision is not personal. It is never done from a personal perspective. These kinds of actions are taken for one reason only: to maintain or improve the size, health, profitability and survival of the company. That's all. As I noted earlier, an active corporation is like a living, breathing entity, and my first loyalty in business is always to it. If the business does not survive, nobody survives. That's the reality that everyone needs to understand and accept.

Several years ago, a business acquaintance gave me some valuable advice. "The bigger your company gets," he said, "the more people you need between yourself and the action of firing someone." It's especially important for business leaders who depend on their charisma as a means of leading their company and its employees. Charismatic people aren't supposed to deliver bad news; it tarnishes their allure. They need other people to do it for them.

Staying close to the sun

The founder and owner of any business becomes the sun, in a manner of speaking, to the employees. He or she is the source of life and energy. Everyone wants to bask in the warmth and glow, and when a company is small and growing, everyone can. The closer an employee is to the sun, the brighter his or her future appears. No matter how challenging things may become, the sun is always shining upon them. Even on cloudy days, to continue the analogy, it is comforting to be close to the source of power. The further people move away from the sun, the darker their outlook.

Keeping the same sense of involvement in the company's goals with 150 employees as you had with five is one of the major challenges of being an entrepreneur. As your company grows, things besides its size begin to change, and making the changes smoothly becomes a serious responsibility.

This reality is another challenge for small businesses evolving into mid-sized and larger operations. Everyone wants to be close to the sun, and as the business grows, the distance between the sun and others in the system becomes wider. The man or woman who founded the company and once sat at a desk next to yours may now be on a higher floor or even in a different location entirely, leaving you in the shade of someone who was not around at the beginning. Some people accept this transition easily. Others don't.

There comes a point in the growth of many companies when the founder and CEO discovers that the time spent finding ways to overcome the challenge of competitors has shrunk to make room for the time to deal with issues involving employees. When this happens, the founder and CEO needs to step back from one activity or the other. The choice to me is always clear. I would far rather invest an hour improving our position against our strongest competitor than spend the same hour pondering how to inform an individual who has contributed a good deal to the company, but is now over his head, that he cannot do the job anymore.

It is easier to study my competition and find ways to attack its weak spot than it is to bring such bad news to an employee.

And infinitely more fun.

17

The 10 Percent Solution

One of the rarest combinations of talent in the business world is an exceptional salesperson who can make the transition to becoming an exceptional manager. It's like someone being equally successful at gymnastics and architecture. It's not impossible, but it sure is unusual. Just think of the brilliant people who managed a company with great success despite lacking the ability to sell an ice machine in the Sahara.

Leadership is another matter. Anyone with outstanding sales ability can achieve almost any goal he or she sets. Selling skills allow extraordinary salespeople to create successful organizations without having equal management abilities. That's because at the heart of all good salespeople are potential leaders who, if they recognize and seize the opportunity, can adapt their sales abilities to leadership duties. And leaders, I submit, are more valuable and important than managers. Why? *Because the most important function of leaders is to inspire those around them,* and the roots of inspiration are based in understanding peoples' needs and desires. My most important role on behalf of my employees and our clients is to provide energy. All successful companies are part machine and part family. On the machine side, I am its primary source of energy. On the family side, I am the keeper and guide of its culture and values. Every successful leader I know subscribes to this concept.

> **"At the heart of all good salespeople are potential leaders."**

It's 90 percent work and 10 percent push

Whether you wish to be a CEO or are content to perform at your best at a lower level in your company, you need to know this: in any successful organization, 90 percent of the employees perform their functions, and the remaining 10 percent drive the company forward. The lesson for business owners is clear: when it comes to motivating, inspiring, supporting and responding, it pays to dedicate most of your energy to the driven 10 percent.

As your company grows, things become more complex in ways you may not expect. When you find that you need more of the 90 percent contingent, they're generally available. But it becomes far more difficult to find people to fill the roles of the critical 10 percent. The more successful you are at hiring these 10 percent and ensuring they play an active role in the company's growth and development, the more successful your organization will be.

This distinction may seem unfair to members of the 90 percent group, most of whom demonstrate all the loyalty, energy and integrity asked of them. But as much as I appreciate the individuals in the 90 percent category, it's a Darwinian fact of life that the members of the 10 percent group determine whether the company succeeds or fails in meeting its objectives. You need the other 90 percent to do their job; just don't count on them being overachievers.

Look at it this way: If you and I were putting together a new NBA team, wouldn't we want to fill the roster with a dozen or so Michael Jordans? Of course we would. But we would be fortunate to find and recruit just one Michael Jordan. And if we did, we would still need a team behind him. In any company, those in the 10 percent group are your Michael Jordans. They represent the foundation around which you build your company and, ultimately, its success.

One of the skills I have drawn upon to reach success in business is adapting my talent for selling to my role as a leader. The most important element of this is my ability to connect with people on their terms and discover what matters to them. This is more important than getting out in front of the people in an organization and saying, "Follow me toward the goal I see just beyond the horizon!" or some similar rallying cry. The goals of the gifted and ambitious people employed at your successful, aggressive business are not likely to be identical to yours, and you should recognize and accept this fact.

I value key people within the Herjavec Group whose personal goals are completely different from my own. Several years ago, a member of the elite U.S. Army Rangers defined a successful team not as a group of people who liked one another, but as people who respected the ability of all the others on the team and were intent on moving toward the same goal. The key word here is "respect." Not everyone has the same personal goals as I have, and not everyone considers me their best friend forever. That's fine with me. It's far more important that we respect each other's abilities and that we share the same objectives. Liking each other is not the issue.

My most important role when it comes to our key employees is to see them as individuals, understand their primary goals and adjust my management style and expectations accordingly. I do this with two people whom I'll call Jim and Jane. Both are among the Michael Jordan group, meaning they are part of the critical 10 percent of employees whose contribution I consider essential to the company's dynamics.

Jim is a major sales success for us. In his mid-30s, he earns a salary in the mid–six figures and, as his income indicates, he works hard. Jim is driven not as much by ambition as by the fear of being unable to provide for his family, including his newborn daughter. I consider his fear unreasonable, but it continues to motivate him and probably will until his children are on their own. The most important aspect of Jim's job to him is an assurance that he will continue being rewarded for his work at his current income level.

Jane is almost 10 years older than Jim. Her concern isn't earning enough money to support herself and her family. It's her belief that she has never had the opportunity to really shine. Time is ticking away for Jane, and she wants the recognition and responsibility she deserves as quickly as possible. Jane needs an environment in which she can stand out and everyone can grasp her skills and abilities.

Jim and Jane each needs a different management style from me, and I try to provide it. Any extra time I take to shape and deliver my approach to them is worth it because it will pay off in better performance for the entire organization.

Some skills are natural, others need development

In some ways, it's easier for me to explain my management abilities than my selling and leadership skills. That's because I had to consciously learn how to be a better manager. I know the steps because I had to follow them and evaluate my progress. I know what worked well for me and what didn't work nearly so well.

I didn't have to learn how to sell and how to lead a team. That came naturally to me. I do both without thinking about the process. I think a lot about how to be a better manager, however, and I feel confident enough to share my ideas about this with you. Not all of them are new, but all are important. Even the best managers, I suspect, need to be reminded from time to time both to apply these ideas and to measure their impact on staff.

If you're a good manager, you are already applying these skills and techniques. If you want to become a good manager, you'll need to learn and practise them.

Positive feedback is essential where earned. Giving positive feedback is one of your key jobs as a manager. You control the amount of feedback delivered to staff, and the more you use feedback successfully, the more staff members will apply it themselves. Positive feedback creates engaged employees who give a damn about their work.

Barriers against bad news are a mistake. Chances are you are not a perfect human being. Neither, I suspect, are your employees.

Honest mistakes will be made, and it's your duty as a manager not only to hear about them but also to correct them when they occur and take steps to prevent them from happening again. Mistakes mean bad news, and people want neither to hear it nor to deliver it. Not hearing bad news is a risk because its impact will arrive when you are unprepared to deal with it. If you're not hearing about mistakes, beware; either your staff isn't trying anything new, or they are afraid to reveal their errors to you.

Trust is better than apathy. Not every idea or proposal you have will be perfect. Something can always be improved or reassessed. The best employees will have the insight and the ambition to make every idea as effective as possible, and may find ways to improve on your concepts or even occasionally express concern about them. Think of both as positive resistance, a means of employees seriously looking for better ways to achieve a common goal. As uncomfortable as this may be to your ego from time to time, learn to develop and treasure an open exchange of ideas and even resistance. Along with the potential of finding better ways to reach your goal, it demonstrates a feeling of trust between you and the critical components of your staff. It is also the best way I know to banish apathy—nothing good comes from apathetic employees.

Cynicism is a deadly disease. Know the difference between positive resistance and cynical response. The first is a nurturing and ultimately uniting force. The second is a shower of cold water dumped on every new idea. Too much cynicism is more than a problem on its own. It is a symptom of morale troubles within the organization, and it demands your attention to find the source and correct it.

Unpleasant surprises are like flashing red lights. When bad news arrives without warning, it indicates one of two things, neither of them encouraging. Either you are dealing with poor communication among your employees or your employees maintain a low level of trust with you. Heed the warning and fix the problem.

Milestones are a big deal. Never let the attainment of your goals become a ho-hum event. Whether the goals are personal, group or corporate, make sure everyone hears about their achievement and celebrates accordingly—even if it's just a matter of sharing high-fives.

Laughter is contagious. You don't need scheduled events or special gestures to create a fun atmosphere. Spontaneous laughter is an immediate measure of a workforce that is loyal, committed and productive. Don't believe me? Picture your employees wearing sullen expressions all day long. Then try to imagine how much energy they're investing in their work.

18

Make No Room for Rumours

I enjoy the public recognition I receive thanks to my appearances on television and the spinoff publicity they generate. But along with a high profile comes the risk of rumours about a number of things, including my business and my private life.

I've managed to avoid the rumour mill in my private life, and I plan to continue to do so, but many celebrities whom I have met deal with rumours day after day. Most of these are silly fluff and a few are laughably out of touch with reality, but some can be seriously hurtful.

Some people in the media try to create negative stories about people in the limelight—like the reporter who refused to believe that I owned a home in Florida and demanded I prove it to her, since she had searched the records without success. I tried to be nice about asserting that, yes, I really did have a home in Florida, but her insistence on finding something negative to say about me and my family—that I had lied about the home—pushed me too far and I hung up on her without explaining that, for privacy reasons,

I had placed the home in the name of a corporate trust. That's why she couldn't locate it on the records. This was hardly a blow to my reputation, and I don't believe it launched any nasty rumours, but it illustrates how far some people will go to find dirt that doesn't exist.

You don't have to be a familiar face to be cautious of rumours. They crop up anywhere people gather and work together, and they are harmful and costly to one extent or another. The root of rumour is gossip, and in a business environment gossip wastes time, damages reputations, creates cliques and destroys morale.

> **" The root of rumour is gossip, and in a business environment gossip wastes time, damages reputations, creates cliques and destroys morale. "**

At the Herjavec Group, we've had our share of rumours about our business, and they always surprise me. The most recent series of rumours involved a firm we purchased in 2011. It was a straight cash deal, not a merger. The company we bought had provided services associated with our industry, but its primary activity was one with which I wasn't completely familiar. I saw many good things about the company but had a few concerns. Overall, however, it appeared worth the tens of millions of dollars it cost to acquire the corporation.

When we purchased companies in the past, we welcomed the new Herjavec Group employees into the family but also explained that, no matter what the systems and procedures they had been following, they had to adapt to ours. We appreciated the effort needed to trade old habits for new ones, but we were also firm about it: their methods may have been interesting, but ours were to be followed. Totally. Our inflexibility was based strictly on practicalities. We didn't want to be dictatorial about it. We just could not have two different ways of doing things within the same corporation. After allowing for a period of adjustment, things eventually smoothed out.

With this newest acquisition, I chose a different approach. The new company employed almost 50 people in five offices across the country, so I agreed that integration would take some time to complete. More important, I was not entirely familiar with that company's corner of the industry, so I was reluctant to dictate immediately that every detail of its operation must fit under the Herjavec umbrella, where systems and procedures were concerned. Deviating from our past policy, I suggested that staff in the newly acquired operation continue working under their previous systems. If they wanted to keep doing things as they had in the past, I was willing to give them time and room to prove their systems were superior to ours in their operation.

As time passed and I learned more about their work and their means of running things, I grew concerned. Some aspects of the company that I had admired were proving to be a problem. It also became clear that basic procedures we followed could be easily implemented by the new company to improve its performance, service and profit.

Meanwhile, much of the feedback I was receiving from key employees of the newly acquired business was anything but encouraging. They openly criticized our way of doing things, scoffed at suggestions on how to make things run more smoothly and were generally derisive of our operations. When I realized my experiment wasn't working, I announced that people in the new division would have to start doing things our way.

My decision met immediate resistance. Okay, no big surprise;

I was suggesting something new and unknown to people who believed they were running things in the best possible manner, and they didn't need me, The New Guy, to suggest otherwise. And when I pointed out that this was not a suggestion but a firm directive to be followed immediately, many of the key people resigned.

When these employees left the company, we had to turn our attention to replacing them with new people who brought similar skill levels to the job. More disturbing was the decision of these four or five former employees to join a direct competitor, where they began spreading rumours that the Herjavec Group was in financial distress and mismanaged. Supposed evidence of my company being mismanaged was the fact that those employees—the source of the rumours—were no longer working there: Why would such enormously talented professionals leave unless their abilities were not being appreciated and their ideas were being rejected?

The rumours were laughable to anyone in possession of the other facts—in part that we were already on our way to doubling our sales volume in the new division for the coming fiscal year. But they were the kind of rumours I did not want circulating among our staff, our customers and the industry generally. We had to deal with them, and we did so by using the following techniques, among others:

Keep the lines of communication open. Rumours tend to fill a vacuum of information; the best way to prevent these vacuums from breeding rumours is to fill them with key information— not fluff designed to make employees feel good but hard facts as they arise. Good communication is especially critical when things don't appear as bright and promising as everyone would hope they were—for instance, when a company downsizes, loses a major account or relocates offices. That's when it's important for everyone to know what is happening, why it is happening, what kind of impact it will make and on whom. Depending on the nature of the news, it could be communicated via a newsletter, weekly meetings or the company's intranet site.

Be open and honest. Sometimes you can't reveal all the information that people would like to know about a situation. Admit this and promise to provide full details as soon as possible. Then be sure to keep your promise. As soon as you can reveal the information, do so—for instance, when a merger will create job redundancies, let employees know the extent to which job losses are expected and the manner in which those who lose their jobs will be compensated.

Maintain as much transparency as possible. The surest way to start rumours and make people feel uncomfortable about their job security is to hold meetings behind closed doors. Yes, sometimes they're necessary. But keep them to a minimum.

Mix with the troops. Finding time to walk around the office, chatting with people about almost anything that comes up, is a great preventer of gossip and rumours. It brings you closer to people you may not normally deal with on a regular basis and provides you with the opportunity to hear about rumours before they grow nasty and destructive.

Let everyone know that rumours are unacceptable in your business. Rumours may be abundant but they needn't be acceptable. Assure employees that if they hear a rumour that seriously affects their job or their personal life, they should feel free to raise it with their supervisor, who will either deal with it or, if need be, take it all the way to the top—to you.

Promote cooperation over competition. When individuals or departments compete for rewards or recognition, it can create a breeding ground for conflict and distrust, leading to gossip and rumours. Competition between departments is generally healthy, but not if it leads to an erosion in morale and productivity.

Prevent rumours—it's easier than eliminating them. I'm not sure any company can completely avoid rumours within the organization. It is possible, however, to minimize rumours through prevention, and to manage them when they arise. Preventing rumours is really a reflection of good management.

19

The Organic Organization

I'm not the first person to recognize a similarity between companies and living organisms. I think I may be one of the most enthusiastic believers in the idea, however. I see businesses as following a path from birth through adolescence and maturity to partnership. They often produce offspring and eventually suffer death from one cause or another, including old age. The good ones have passion, the exceptional ones have purpose and all are subject to ailments such as hubris, smugness and arthritic immobility. Sure sounds like people to me . . .

> **" I see businesses as following a path from birth through adolescence and maturity to partnership. "**

When you examine the needs of living organisms, including corporations and human beings, from a psychologist's standpoint, it becomes almost a management course in itself. The best illustration of this is Maslow's theory, which describes the hierarchy of needs, an idea developed back in the 1940s.

Marketing professionals use it as the basis for many of their strategies and tactics.

Maslow's theory, named for American psychologist Abraham Maslow, is designed to identify the process leading to self-actualization, defined as an inner need to become everything that an individual is capable of becoming. It's all a matter of fulfilling your potential by meeting goals you set for yourself.

The theory encompasses five levels of needs, and you proceed to the next level only when you have satisfied all the needs of the current level. Also, within each macro level is a hierarchy of individual levels that must be satisfied in turn. Here are the five levels. As you read them, imagine the needs applying to a business organization as well as to yourself.

Level 1: Physiological Needs

Air, water, food, shelter, sleep

Level 2: Safety Needs

Protection, security, order, stability

Level 3: Belonging Needs

Family, friendship, community, work relationships

Level 4: Esteem Needs

Respect, status, achievement, recognition

Level 5: Self-actualization Needs

Personal growth and fulfilment

The first level covers all the physical requirements of an organism. Without air, the organism doesn't survive. Without food and water, it wastes away. Without shelter, it succumbs to exposure and the elements.

Once the physical needs are met, the organism looks for ways to protect itself and ensure its longevity, moving to the second level. Safety becomes a primary concern, along with a need for a reliable supply of food and other essential resources of the first level.

With basic physiological and safety requirements met, the needs grow psychological in nature. What's the point of merely existing if you lack friends, companions and reassurance that you really matter in the grand scheme of things? The organism begins to seek love and esteem, goals that fill levels 3 and 4.

Level 5 is at the top of the needs hierarchy, the place where all living creatures with personal consciousness and identity want to be. At this level they are easily distinguishable from other creatures around them, the ones competing for all the resources on the lower levels.

Now apply this analogy to corporations. They need a location with facilities to carry on their business—offices, factories and warehouses fit here on the first level. Next comes obtaining security and safety, creating an atmosphere in which to do business free of immediate and fatal risks.

When organisms reach the third level, they begin looking beyond themselves. In corporations, this becomes a vital step toward expansion and consolidation among customers and suppliers. Eventually, the organization grows comfortable with its identity, with the goals it has accomplished and with the esteem it has created among its customers and its competition.

Fewer companies than we may think reach the final level of the hierarchy. "Self-actualization" is a 10-dollar word for "fulfil-ment." In a business environment it identifies any company that has achieved sufficient power and confidence to set its own goals and standards independent of others, and use these new goals to foster its continued expansion.

Perhaps the biggest lesson in applying Maslow's theory to busi-ness activities is that the final level is not a place to lie down and relax (for one thing, there's not much room up there). When a company manages to reach this level, it can't stop progressing, and it can't stop fending off competition attempting to rise up from the lower levels.

Think of companies you know whose histories reflect the hier-archy. Some firms are content to never move past level 3. Unable or unwilling to make the necessary connections, they remain both local and limited. Others may grow in size, but their progress through the levels is limited by less-than-spotless reputations or poor image problems. And still others make it to the final level of the hierarchy only to be pushed back a level or two because they are unable to handle the challenge of competition.

No better example of Maslow's theory exists as a model for business than Research In Motion, creator of the BlackBerry. For years the name was practically synonymous with advanced com-munication, towering over other companies that lacked its esteem, confidence and connections. Eventually RIM was knocked aside by competitors ready to claim the top level as their own. RIM retains substantial credibility and industry recognition, enough that it may yet reclaim its peak position, but until then, its esteem won't make much impact on its bottom line or future growth. It will take creativity, knowledge and aesthetic qualities, all bundled in the same manner that once generated market mystique and produced spectacular growth and fulfilment for the company.

Systems in organisms and organizations

Scientists classify organisms into species, and at last count an estimated 10 million species had been identified, ranging from penguins in Antarctica to crocodiles in equatorial Africa. I'll bet there are at least that many active businesses in operation around the world at any one time. Each successful species knows how to make the most of its environment, and the most successful organisms down through history have learned to adapt to major changes in their environments. Those that were unable to change became extinct.

Together with Maslow's hierarchy of needs, this led me to write down a few guidelines to use when applying the metaphor of corporations as living organisms.

There is no one "best way" of designing and managing an organization. All functioning organizations/organisms operate at optimum efficiency within their own industry environment. Change the environment and the organization/organism either changes or dies.

Organizations/organisms depend on the efficient flow of systems. In sophisticated organisms, key systems carry nutrients needed for survival. In organizations, the major systems carry information and cash.

All organizations/organisms must optimize the fit between individuals and resources. Birds need strong wings more than powerful legs. Worms need neither. The fit between function and environment must be addressed.

All internal changes must be made and assessed against changes in the external environment. Changes—structural, organizational, financial and so on—made to suit internal perceptions without regard to external reality generate neither advantages nor benefits.

All elements of an organization/organism must change in response to major changes in the environment. Failure to adapt may lead to the obliteration of the element through atrophy, or to the demise of the entire organism.

20

Knowing without Knowing How You Know

I have a theory about intuition—how we acquired it as humans, and how successfully we use it. Anthropologists, psychologists and various others may shoot holes in my idea, but I suspect that successful people in business will nod their heads in agreement with me, to at least some extent anyway. Here's my theory.

Eons ago, our Stone Age ancestors frequently had to travel some distance to obtain food, leaving the relative comfort and security of their caves. Whenever food was not available within the immediate area of their home or their settlement, the hunters had to venture beyond the adjacent land in search of nourishment to sustain themselves and their families, which meant entering unseen territory harbouring unknown risks and dangers. Sometimes they travelled with other tribes or in loose groupings, using teamwork to capture their prey and sharing it among themselves. The group also served to protect individuals against attacks from strangers who might be encountered along the way.

The hunters were not always the predators. Sometimes they were the prey for four-legged animals performing the same action to fulfil the same need. Some hunters were better than others at sensing both prey and danger, meaning they tended to be more successful at bringing food to their families. They were more likely to survive than those with less responsive senses, so they were also more successful at having descendants and passing along this trait to them. The more their descendants inherited and applied this talent, the better they were at producing their own offspring, who also inherited and applied it, generation after generation.

It's not as complicated as Darwin's theory, but you can see where I am going with this.

Success always involves taking risks

The most successful people in any enterprise are the ones who venture beyond the comfort of their cave in search of something better across the next river and over the next hill. Yes, it's where danger lies. It's also where opportunities are found. The fattest cattle and richest harvest are rarely within sight of your cave. The cave dwellers who possessed both sharp intuition and the willingness to take risks lived longer and produced more and healthier offspring, who then passed these traits down to their own descendants. I suspect they also passed along another survival trait: intuition.

I am a firm believer in the value of education and experience. I am equally firm in my belief that anyone who sneers at or belittles the value of intuition in setting career goals and making business decisions is in danger of being gobbled up by a sabre-tooth tiger somewhere over the next hill.

Those who possess a high degree of intuitive insight rarely discuss it because it's difficult to define and explain. MBA studies may cover a wide range of skills and applications, but they are never likely to elevate the intuition levels among students who lack them. Bragging about intuitive skills is not the kind of thing that a board chairperson or CEO tells shareholders when explaining why and how a decision was made to merge with another company, or to introduce a new product. These kinds of decisions are expected to be based on logic, but logic can take you only so far down the road toward a decision.

This kind of intuition is also called "street smarts," and I am often amazed at the number of MBA grads who brag about the knowledge they gained from books without acknowledging that they're seriously short of street smarts.

When Mark Cuban, Daymond John and I were asked to speak to a group of business students at Harvard, we realized that none of us had an MBA. Daymond barely finished high school, and Mark and I barely finished university. We were all short on "book smarts," but if we were to take a course in street smarts, we would graduate summa cum laude.

> "The most successful people in any enterprise are the ones who venture beyond the comfort of their cave in search of something better across the next river and over the next hill."

I'm all in favour of higher education and I'll insist on my children attending university, but I also believe that too many people place too much stress on their children earning the right degree from the right university, even if it creates a mountain of debt for the student or the parents. No university course I know can teach intuition. The best way I know of to learn street smarts is to get out into the world and get your hands dirty.

Intuition is knowing without knowing how you know

Scientists call intuition "immediate cognition," which to me sounds like the same thing. Intuition, when blended with the right-brain characteristics of creativity and humour, has been identified as a key factor in the ability of an individual to solve difficult problems and reach defined goals.

One of the challenges of describing intuition is the fact that it carries so many labels, depending who is using it, and how. I call the skill my spider senses; fans of Spider-Man movies prefer "spidey senses." This sounds too casual for business leaders, and maybe too creepy for people suffering from arachnophobia. On a professional level, the term "integrative presence" is often used, suggesting feelings and actions built on ego and insecurity rather than wisdom and experience. "Integrative presence" is a bit academic for me, but it lifts the discussion off the comics page.

Wisdom and experience would tell the prehistoric hunter—and the aggressive business person—that deer or buffalo or some other protein on the hoof would be visiting a nearby waterhole at a certain time of day, and that they represented a promising source of food. But during the hunt it was ego and insecurity that maintained the hunter's sensitivity to sights, sounds and smells that represented danger, when the hunter was unable to rationalize them or even confirm their presence.

Professional athletes use a specialized form of intuition they call "being in the zone." It's that feeling that occurs when the world appears to slow down and everything around you blurs except the one thing that holds your attention, that matters to you beyond everything else in life at that moment. Ask a Major League Baseball player or National Hockey League player to describe this state and he'll respond with words like "exhilarated," "confident" and "powerful." Yet none of these words really describes the state athletes enter when making an outstanding play at a critical point in a game or match, especially those when the championship rides on that athlete's success or failure.

Those who succeed under intense pressure and are later asked how they managed to score that winning home run or make the basketball shot with five seconds left on the clock often refer to a unique sense of time. The home-run hitter may recall that the baseball appeared to hang waiting for the bat to be swung; the basketball player may say that the five seconds seemed to last five minutes, giving him all the time in the world to set up the shot—to determine the arc for the ball to follow, the height that he needed to jump and the twist he gave to avoid the defending guard. To the other players and all the spectators, however, each event occurred as quickly and brilliantly as lightning.

Professional sports are played in highly charged environments, but many business decisions are made in quiet, contemplative moments when the decision maker needs to reflect on all that he or she knows. Making a decision without using one's own intuition, however, is rarely a wise move. Rick George, former CEO of Suncor Energy, described a decision he made in the mid-1990s to commit his company to spending almost $3 billion on an expansion program. In addition to investing substantially more than the entire capitalized value of the company at the time, George made the decision at a period when Suncor's product, crude oil drawn from the Alberta oil sands, was selling at $12 per barrel. Reliable sources were forecasting that the price could fall as low as $5 per barrel, yet Suncor needed a price of $50 simply to break even.

Many within the petroleum industry openly scoffed at George's decision, suggesting that Suncor was doomed to sink within its enormous liability and vanish out of sight. Logic, they claimed, did not support spending that much money on such an outrageous risk. They pointed out that the total capitalization of the company when George assumed the CEO position just a few years earlier had been less than a billion dollars. Now he intended to commit nearly three times that much on an expansion program during a depressed market. Was he mad?

George wasn't mad. He had calculated the risk. He had applied his intuition, which had never failed him in the past. He had also refused to blindly follow the herd, no matter in what direction it was stampeding. At the time, the herd was shrinking its investment and activities in the oil patch, anticipating the low prices to remain that way indefinitely.

"Good management is not about the state of things as they are today," George has explained. "It's about the state of things as they will be tomorrow."* Intuition told him that oil prices would not remain at such a low ebb, and they didn't. By the time the expansion program was completed, oil prices had risen well inside Suncor's profit territory. And by the time George retired, the value of Suncor had climbed to more than $70 billion, making it the second largest capitalized corporation in the country.

Despite this and other examples, many people choose not to trust their intuition. They may even seek opinions of others, opinions that are in direct conflict with their spider senses, not to test the validity of their intuition but to search for a consensus they can cling to. In other words, they want to follow the same herd ignored by people like Rick George. And by me.

Whenever my spider senses start guiding me toward a decision, I put my subconscious to work on it. I fill my head with as much information as I need, listen closely to my spider senses and get a good night's rest—which to me is about four or five hours of deep sleep. If my spider senses are still tingling the next morning, I follow wherever they appear to be leading me.

They have never let me down.

---

* For the complete story of Rick George's successful growth program and other achievements at Suncor Energy, see *Sun Rise: Suncor, the Oil Sands, and the Future of Energy* (Toronto: HarperCollins, 2012).

Things to trust about your spider senses

If you assume that your spider senses are as much a part of your identity as your athletic ability or your inherent musical skills, it follows that they can be sharpened and developed. Practice helps, but it's more important to maintain trust in your intuition's ability to guide you forward. Here are five points about your spider senses to remember to help you keep the faith:

They are as unique as you are. They may or may not mesh entirely with the intuition of others, but they will always be true to your individual goals and perception.

They complement your reason. They are made more powerful when you blend them with your ability to analyze and deduce, the experience you have collected over your career and the information you have at hand.

They are unemotional. Intuition cannot and must not reflect any purely emotional motive like love, anger or revenge. If you believe these are driving your decision, it is not intuition you are hearing; it is some other voice that must be silenced. This can be a challenge. I have long believed that we are not thinking machines that feel but emotional machines that think. Sometimes you need to get your ego out of the way, and sometimes you can let your competitor's ego take over and make a mistake that benefits you.

They demand action. They are not academic or contemplative. Think back to the cave dwellers and all the dangers they faced the further they ventured from their shelter. Intuition tells you, "Do something!" Sometimes making a good decision today is preferable to making a perfect decision tomorrow.

They should always be listened to. They are not always infallible. But they should never be ignored.

Finally, if you don't buy my opinion about the value of intuition, maybe Einstein's will carry a little more weight. Here's what he reportedly said on the subject: "The intuitive mind is a sacred gift, and the rational mind is a faithful servant. We have created a society that honours the servant and has forgotten the gift."

21

The Most Important Part of Listening

The concept of *Shark Tank* is brilliant, a fact proven by the show's continued success. But I've learned something that veterans in the entertainment business recognize immediately: it's the manner in which the show is produced and directed that makes all the difference between a good concept and a hit show.

One of the things that I and the other Sharks have learned is the importance of listening quietly to build drama during the show. We all know the importance of listening, of course. None of us would have achieved the success we have if we hadn't acquired this skill. But sometimes when a pitcher is becoming carried away with his or her deal, or has run out of things to offer us, we remain silent. None of us speaks. The silence generates drama, and encourages the pitcher to rethink what he or she has said, or elevates the sense of urgency. It's an effective, almost theatrical technique, and it's one that can be used, with a little modification and a lot of care, in any business situation.

The next time you watch *Shark Tank,* look for the moment

when all five of us say nothing and simply gaze at the presenter, waiting for him or her to speak. The pause may last only two or three seconds (it may have been longer during the show's taping, but too much silence is dreaded "dead air" in broadcasting, so it is often shortened during the editing stage), but to the presenter it seems endless. Their expression reads "Somebody say something!" But in the end, he or she is the one who speaks first, usually taking the pitch in a new and potentially exciting direction.

> " **The most important part of listening involves remaining silent.** "

That's the power of silence, a power that too few people make use of in business and personal relationships. I'm not referring to the silence of disdain or a cold shoulder, but to the interval in a conversation that permits both sides to arrange their thoughts before they speak.

By the way, I'm intrigued that the same letters from the alphabet are used in the word *silent* and in the word *listen.* Perhaps it's evidence that the most important part of listening involves remaining silent.

The subtle communication of silence

Silence is implied in listening, but it's also an important part of speaking, because silence is where the words coalesce to make an impact. If you think back to meetings you've attended, especially raucous ones such as a town hall gathering where everyone feels their opinion is the only one worth listening to, or a business meeting conducted under great pressure, you'll likely recall that the critical views were often made following a period of silence and reflection. In my experience, any meeting that is an endless series of statements and rebuttals with no opportunity for reflection and response doesn't achieve much.

We may initially think that nothing is being communicated if no one is speaking. But that's not true. Our ability to communicate with precise words is one of the qualities that defines us as human beings, we do not always depend upon words alone. Whether we are consciously aware of their impact or not, things like body language, facial expressions and the subtleties of speaking—inflection, tone, rhythm—deliver their own messages. With verbal communication, it is not always necessary, or even desirable, to string a bunch of words together in a continuous unbroken chain. That kind of chatter is very good for diverting an audience's attention, but it's not productive when it comes to expressing ideas and emotions clearly. We can also communicate very effectively not with words, but with carefully selected periods of silence.

The jazz genius Miles Davis was once asked why his music stood out among that of others, and why people absorbed so much feeling and emotion from it. His answer, I'll bet, was confusing to some and enlightening to others, including me. "It's because," he said, "I play the spaces between the notes."

Spaces between the notes? How can you play music where no music exists? It may take a little reflection to understand that Davis meant he gave as much thought and attention to the time spent *not* playing a note as he did to playing the notes themselves. He created silence to build anticipation for the next note, and the location and length of the silence—a fraction of a beat here and several beats elsewhere—became as much a part of the music as the sound of his trumpet. I'm no musician, so I can't fully appreciate all the technical aspects of what he did, but I grasped the idea. You might keep this concept in mind the next time you make a speech or presentation. Give as much consideration to the spaces between words as to the words themselves, and watch how it improves the impact of your message.

> " Give as much consideration to the spaces between words as to the words themselves, and watch how it improves the impact of your message. "

Being the first to speak is not necessarily an advantage

As someone who enjoys public speaking, I have had to learn the value of remaining silent as a means of communicating well. Applying this knowledge successfully takes a bit of practice and a lot of experience, but I've come across a few tricks that have proven effective over the years.

For example, I try to avoid being the first person to make a comment in a meeting. If it's my meeting, I'm the first to speak, of course, but I've learned that the fourth or fifth person to speak often has more to contribute. This makes sense. After listening carefully to the first three or four speakers, you have both knowledge of the context of the discussion and an opportunity to tailor your comments according to the situation. You know the other side's position, you sense the attitude of others in the room and you frame your words accordingly.

When the time comes for your contribution, remember the value of silence, even interspersed with your comments. Silence provides an opportunity to organize your thoughts and choose your words to make your point as specifically as possible. Silence between sentences also builds an expectation on the part of listeners. It sharpens their listening powers by generating a certain amount of suspense.

You don't need to pause very long; just two or three seconds will do. That's long enough for the listener to subconsciously prepare to give your next words more weight than if you burst out speaking immediately.

> **" Silence between sentences also builds an expectation on the part of listeners. It sharpens their listening powers by generating a certain amount of suspense. "**

I also believe that we tend to award our trust to people who do not speak immediately but who appear to dedicate some thought to the words they plan to deliver.

I recall hearing about a tactic used by the film director John Houston when he was creating his great film *The Man Who Would Be King.* The movie stars Sean Connery and Michael Caine, who play two British soldiers planning to steal a fortune from a kingdom in a remote corner of northern India. The two men are brash and foolhardy, especially Peachy, Michael Caine's character. To emphasize this aspect of Peachy's personality, Houston instructed Caine to deliver his lines before others finished speaking, overlapping conversations if necessary. Peachy was impetuous, not reflective or thoughtful, and Houston wanted Caine's delivery of his dialogue to create that quality.

It was good direction. Caine's character appears exactly as he should in the film, expressing his thoughts without weighing them first, and the characteristic adds to the movie's believability.

Houston's advice illustrates the importance of pausing before speaking if you want to be viewed as a thoughtful and considerate person.

It's a matter of balancing reason and emotion. Emotion is the force that urges you to respond to something immediately. One of the most important things I have had to learn is to control my emotions when speaking. Like most entrepreneurs, I am proud of my achievements, and when I feel slighted, I want to speak up and make my point immediately. It takes self-control to remain quiet and assess things before speaking. Sometimes the hardest person to control in a meeting is yourself.

Of course, when the emotion is positive, you can and should respond enthusiastically immediately. After all, nobody sits for several minutes after hearing good news before standing and shouting "Hooray!" When your reaction is less positive, even critical and condemning, it makes sense to consider your response before delivering it. I guarantee you will never be asked to take back a compliment, but you may wish you could retract something unflattering you said to another person, especially in the presence of others.

In a meeting or discussion, try to be aware of those two qualities, reason and emotion. Make use of the first, and keep the second in check. You don't have to leap to your feet to express your support, and you shouldn't immediately make a negative comment about any suggestion either.

If it helps, keep in mind the guiding principle of the Jesuits: reason over passion. They didn't banish the idea of passion from discourse. They just put it in its place.

22

Branding—It's Not Just for Cattle

Among one of the least acknowledged but most influential developments in business these days is personal branding. Not the kind that's done with a red-hot iron on cattle (I'll do a lot to build my business, but that's where I draw the line). I'm referring to branding techniques that were once reserved exclusively for products and are now more and more frequently being applied to individuals in and out of show business.

The ability of some savvy and distinct marketers to use branding as an immensely powerful sales tool is growing more refined. Some brands are so strong that they leverage people into making buying decisions without regard for other factors. I know, because I have been the target of that strategy, and guess what? It worked.

The power of a prestigious brand

Two years ago I purchased a Ferrari 458. The car is designed exclusively for racing, though it does offer a passenger seat for coaches to occupy during training sessions. I love the car so much that when I heard Ferrari planned to introduce a Super car in 2013, I told my Ferrari dealer to add my name to the waiting list.

Ferrari introduces a new Super model every few years, with a limited production run. The last Super was the Enzo, introduced in 2002. Only 399 Enzos were produced, and all but 50 of them were manufactured only after Ferrari owners had placed their orders.

Buying a Ferrari is not quite the same as buying a Ford Fusion. When Ferrari makes a Super car, you don't call the dealer to buy one; Ferrari invites you to purchase one. This way, the company manufactures fewer cars than there are buyers, which is part of its branding and marketing strategy. In order to buy a Ferrari Super, you request to be put on the list of people whom Ferrari has invited to buy the model when it becomes available. If this sounds like the same system used to make a dinner reservation at a popular restaurant . . . well, it's not.

This newest Super, I learned, would be something very special, even for a Ferrari. With a V12 engine delivering almost 1000 horsepower, the new model would have the usual Ferrari sex appeal, plus a series of new cutting-edge technical advances, including carbon-fibre construction and electronic control systems.

When I asked my dealership to put my name on the list, it was pleased to do so. No promises are made, of course. Your name goes on the list, and you are called if and when your car arrives. The procedure is different from when you first join the club of Ferrari owners. At that point, all it takes to buy a Ferrari is writing a fat cheque. If you've ordered a California, the least expensive Ferrari currently available, you'll hand over about $230,000 and leave in a two-seater roadster with a 4.3-litre eight-cylinder engine, a seven-speed manual transmission and the glory (there's no other word for it) of driving the world's best sports car.

I placed my order for a Super, then went on to other things. Later I read that Ferrari was introducing an entirely new car, the FF model. It would be the first Ferrari with both four-wheel drive and seating for four people. It sounded like a cross between an SUV and a sedan—but it was a Ferrari with a 12-cylinder, 660-horsepower engine! This was too much to resist, even at $340,000, so I ordered one. Unlike acquiring a Ferrari Super, this involved no selection process. I had the money, I was a previous Ferrari buyer, so I would get the car. In fact, I was informed that I would be taking delivery of the first FF model available in Canada.

No company understands the allure and branding of its product better than Ferrari. In an interview I read some time ago, the CEO of Ferrari was asked how many of a certain type of model he was going to produce. His answer: "Exactly one less than the market will want."

Every powerful brand succeeds by representing the sum of all the valuable qualities of the product to the consumer. For those who enjoy driving sports cars, as I do, Ferrari represents the pinnacle of the science. The sum of all its valuable qualities promotes Ferrari to its admittedly limited consumer base, supporting and in many ways creating buyer demand.

> " Every powerful brand succeeds by representing the sum of all the valuable qualities of the product to the consumer. "

Ferrari has been successful at making grown men with sufficient assets act like little girls giddy with excitement over a new doll. I can't imagine this technique working with other products, but for the car whose logo is a prancing horse, and whose lines and performance are practically a sexual thrill in themselves, it works very well.

How much is your name worth? Coca-Cola's is worth $72 billion

The value of a strong brand has been recognized since someone first hung a name on whatever item he or she produced. Over time, brands acquire personality and character, and they represent something that the owners can use to promote the recognition and sale of their products.

Creating and protecting an established brand pays off. No company in the world has been more concerned about protecting and enhancing its brand than Coca-Cola. I looked into the estimated value of brand names around the world and discovered that Coca-Cola's name alone has been valued at almost $72 billion.* In every corner of the world, the name "Coca-Cola" calls up an image of a cold, dark, sweet, fizzy drink. Beyond that, it also brings to mind a long-established company with a warm and friendly persona.

Similar images, carefully structured and promoted by their brands' owners, are associated with names such as McDonald's, Disney and Gillette, rated among the top 20 most valued brands. No surprise there.

---

* Interbrand, *2011 Ranking of the Top 100 Brands.*

I was somewhat amazed, however, to discover brand names not normally associated with consumer buying decisions sitting high on the most-valued list among Coca-Cola and McDonald's—brands like Intel (7th), HP (10th), Cisco (13th), Nokia (14th) and Oracle (20th). These brands may be familiar, but unless you are as closely associated with computer and Internet technology as I am, your identification with them is not as intimate as it is with a brand like Pepsi (which failed to make the top 20 listing, by the way).

The purpose of building your brand is to attract and support your customers—no one else. People spend too much time creating a brand for people who will never buy their products. It may make you feel good to have your brother-in-law recognize your company name and logo, but if he's not a prime customer, it doesn't do you any good. The first rule of branding is to know your customers and target them specifically. Oracle does not need every consumer between ages 8 and 80 to know its product in the same way that Coke does. Spend your marketing money on the people you need to know you. The process demands a sniper rifle, not a shotgun.

The value of good branding is often underestimated. Intel, whose brand is promoted by hardware manufacturers using their products, scored a brand value of over $35 billion, slightly behind McDonald's and ahead of Apple. Remember—the $35 billion has no connection with product, real estate, patents, inventory or any other tangible asset. It is merely the value of the name. It's possible that if you offered Intel $35 billion and it agreed to sell, you could slap the name on anything you chose and Intel would begin calling itself Acme Memory Inc.

In the age of instant access and global marketing, creating a carefully constructed brand is no longer restricted to the kinds of products purchased by a vast number of consumers every day. It conveys value at various levels and in different product categories, and it can apply to people as effectively (or as disastrously) as it does to products. The idea that a brand can apply to people too grows more powerful every year. You know what you like about and what you expect from Coca-Cola and Chevrolet; you probably also have specific responses when you hear the name Jennifer Aniston. Or Robert Herjavec.

Two different Sharks, two different brands

My experiences on *Dragons' Den* and *Shark Tank,* and my encounters with celebrities ranging from Oprah to Sylvester Stallone, have changed my opinion of personal branding. I used to think that as long as you just sit in the corner and are good at what you do, you don't have to climb on the rooftops to shout how great you are. Now, however, I believe your personal brand is important no matter who you are, even if you're a mid-level manager. Sure, it's fine to be good, but it's better to have people know your special talents and what you stand for. In my first book, I referred to this idea as "humble arrogance"—you have to be bold

> "I believe your personal brand is important no matter who you are."

enough to let the world know who you are, yet not be so arrogant that nobody wants to spend time with you.

Daymond John is widely considered one of the most sought-after branding experts in the business. He actively walks, talks and effectively sells FUBU, his brand of urban clothing, while positioning himself as "The Godfather of Urban Fashion." He also offers a clear definition of branding. If your brand is good, Daymond told me, people know who you are and what you stand for before you show up. If your brand is great, it matches people's expectations when they meet you.

Daymond also believes that you should be able to describe your personal brand in six words or less. This is more difficult than it sounds. Mine could be: "Internet security provider who has fun."

> " Choosing inherent aspects of your personality to enhance and focus upon is an effective way of building a personal brand and using it to help achieve your goals. "

The higher your ambitions and the more you wish to achieve in your career, the more attention you should pay to developing and maintaining your brand— the combination of personality, character and skills you present to the world.

This may appear contrived at first glance. With some people, it is. Pretending you are a paragon of virtue and a pillar of trust when your actions actually tilt toward sociopathic tendencies inevitably leads to disaster. But choosing inherent aspects of your personality to enhance and focus upon is an effective way of building a personal brand and using it to help achieve your goals.

Kevin O'Leary dedicates as much of his time and energy to building his brand as any corporation I know. In case you're not aware of it, Kevin's brand is built on greed and intimidation. His only criterion for assessing an individual, a corporation or an investment opportunity is the amount of money he can expect to make. Kevin famously says, "It's always about the money." Love him or hate him, the man is a master of building his personal brand. It works because Kevin understands that great brands are true to and consistent with the image presented to the public or market.

No viewer of *Shark Tank* could possibly confuse Kevin with any other panellist, nor could they claim they don't know what he stands for. His brand is crystal clear. Some people are turned off by Kevin's overriding emphasis on money and his bullying of people on the show, including sometimes his fellow Sharks. Others love his aggressive attitude, his declaration that he delivers "the truth" and his designation of himself as "Mister Wonderful." The fact is (and Kevin may deny it, but it's true), when he is out of the spotlight, Kevin can be something of a pussycat. He tries to hide this soft side because it conflicts with the public's perception of his brand.

In case it need be said, I could not possibly build that kind of personal brand for myself. For one thing, both my values and my personality are worlds apart from Kevin's. And for another, I can't be cynical. I am as aware of the benefits of branding as anyone, but I prefer it to be based entirely on natural qualities and not be contrived in any manner. None of the panellists on *Shark Tank* is able to portray one brand publicly and be a completely different person once the cameras stop rolling. If we could, we would be actors, not investors. This is one reason why the show works so well: what you see is what you get (except for Kevin).

Should you be building a personal brand? Maybe you already are.

The idea of any individual other than a politician or a movie star creating a personal brand would have sounded ridiculous a generation ago. Today, like it or not, everyone can establish a brand to some degree or another, although this identity is usually limited to their immediate family and friends. Social media has made all the difference. Facebook and Twitter have become, for individuals, akin to billboards and packaging for consumer products in our parents' day. Today, everyone using social media is concerned about the face, the attitude, the political beliefs and other qualities they present to the world—even if "the world" is limited to a dozen or so people who check their Facebook page now and then.

Should you make a conscious effort to develop your personal brand beyond whatever you post (or don't post) on Facebook? It depends on your personal goals and your comfort level about promoting yourself. If thinking of yourself as a brand provides the opportunity to sharpen the positive impression you make on your boss, your colleagues and your customers, it's already worthwhile. Try it.

Here are some tips to build and enhance your personal brand. These ideas are most effective for leaders and CEOs who are prominent within their organization and in the public eye, but should prove valuable to some extent to everyone.

Determine your strengths and goals. You can't build a successful brand out of thin air. It must be built on tangible differences and draw the attention of the people whom you want to respond to your brand. If you're somewhat introverted and prefer reading a book to partying all night long, forget about trying to appear brash and impulsive. There is a place for thoughtful, reflective people; occupy it.

Be authentic. If you're not a natural salesperson and have little interest in focusing exclusively on selling, don't try to build your brand around that particular skill. If the brand you're considering makes you uncomfortable, it's wrong— find another one.

Reflect your brand visually. People associate personal talents with their owner's appearance. Advertising agencies expect their creative staff to dress and groom themselves differently from account executives. Their clients assume that people who wear jeans and funky hairstyles are more creative than those in tailor-made suits and polished shoes. And have you ever encountered a corporate lawyer dressed in Levis and sneakers while at the office? Not likely.

Use social networking to establish your brand. I'm a big user of Twitter. In my postings I mention achievements and observations that reinforce my appearances both on and off the TV shows, as well as my racing schedule and, of course, my company's work. Other networking opportunities include Facebook and LinkedIn.

Use your brand as a platform for ideas. No one has been more effective in establishing and capitalizing on his personal brand than Richard Branson. His smiling bearded face is that of someone to whom success appears inevitable. There seem to be no limits to the challenges he chooses to assume, and whatever happens, he is having the time of his life. That's Branson's brand and, while you are unlikely to match him in the expanse of enterprises he has launched, you can learn a great deal from his success as a personal brand.

Make your name known. Set up a website with your name as part of the address. Offer to submit articles on an aspect of your business to local media, with your name in the byline. Inform the media of your availability as an interview source on topics that you want associated with your brand. Consider taking courses on public speaking and media relations, if you feel you need them. Some of the most effective techniques to use when giving a speech or being interviewed by the media are remarkable easy to grasp and apply—for instance, gesturing with your hands, pausing for a beat or two between sentences and using notes to make your delivery sound more like a conversation than a corporate report.

Be consistent. Deliver the same message and image no matter who the audience or what the circumstances.

23

Don't Get Stuck Halfway up the Mountain

The question "What's the difference between me and very wealthy and successful people?" is usually followed by "I work hard, I think I'm intelligent and I know I'm ambitious. So why can't I live in a big house and drive expensive cars and mingle with celebrities?"

No matter who asks this question, my answer always comes down to the same core: risk.

There is no reward without risk. The problem is that most people can't embrace risk. In fact, they spend a good part of their life avoiding it. Which may be one of the reasons immigrants to North America succeed to such an impressive extent. When you leave your homeland, as my parents did, to start a new life in a country where you are unfamiliar with the people, the language, the social customs and virtually everything else you'll encounter, you have already taken a major risk. Taking a few more to reach success is relatively easy.

You don't have to be an immigrant to understand the value of risk-taking, of course. It's not your country of origin that counts as much as your state of mind. If you feel the most important thing in your life is to hang on to as many of the material comforts you have acquired as possible, you might as well enjoy them because they will likely be all you'll attain in life.

A reasonable definition of success

Let's be clear once again: all of the people I have met who have achieved a level of economic success similar to my own were driven to realize a dream, but not necessarily to become wealthy. Remember, success is doing what you want to do. If you want to be the best teacher in your school system, the best watercolour painter in your art class or the best golfer among your club membership and you achieve that status, you are successful, and I have great respect for you.

> **Instead of thinking of success and failure as seats on different ends of a teeter-totter, think of them as two sides of a coin—you carry both in your pocket at the same time.**

Most people who ask for my advice are aiming higher than that. Along with satisfying whatever drive they have to succeed, they're hoping for the by-products of wealth and recognition that go with it. While they may be mature enough to recognize that no magic formula for success exists, they assume that hard work alone, with perhaps an injection of good luck, is all they need.

Well, not quite.

It's easy to visualize success and failure at opposite points of the spectrum, like black and white or hot and cold. But that's not the way it is. Instead of thinking of success and failure as seats on different ends of a teeter-totter, think of them as two sides of a coin—you carry both in your pocket at the same time.

I'm not suggesting that the risk needed to achieve success is based on flipping that coin and hoping it lands with success facing up more often than failure. That's a gambler's trap, and neither I nor anyone I know who has achieved similar levels of success made it through gambling.

Life isn't a matter of flipping a coin over and over. It's a matter of climbing a mountain, with the ultimate prize waiting at the top. Assuming you want the prize badly enough, you start climbing, taking calculated risks along the way. You plot each step, consider each hand-hold, and measure each crevasse to make sure you can leap safely to the other side, always with your eye on that prize at the peak.

> " Life isn't a matter of flipping a coin over and over. It's a matter of climbing a mountain, with the ultimate prize waiting at the top. "

Each step you take and each metre you climb brings you closer either to success or failure. (This analogy works, by the way, whether we're talking about career planning or personal relationships.)

There comes a time, so I'm told (I have not been tempted to try mountain climbing myself), when climbers on their way to the top reach a critical juncture and are faced with three options. The first is to retreat, having decided that the barrier cannot be overcome, either abandoning entirely your goal of reaching the peak or returning to ground level for a reassessment of the effort. The second is to take a calculated risk, accepting the fact that if you fail to jump the chasm or the rock you are about to grab breaks away in your hand, you will fall.

The third option, I hear, is all too common among novices or those who are not fully committed to success, and it is to do nothing. In a word, you freeze. Unable or unwilling to back down, and unable to take the risk that will keep you moving ever upward, you cling to the mountain, refusing to change your footing and grip. You remain somewhere in the limbo between total success and ultimate failure; one is inaccessible, the other intolerable. You will remain hanging on for dear life because it appears to be the only safe response, and you will stay where you are until either you are rescued or you die, frozen mid-mountain, unable to make the move that could lead to the success you dreamed about when you began the climb.

Once again, action is better than inaction. If you stay on the mountain and do nothing, you will freeze to death.

Know the line between determination and foolish obsession

I don't want to appear harsh toward people who avoid risk. It is their life, not mine, and no one should assume the right to judge the life decisions of another. Nor am I suggesting that success can be achieved only by risking everything in a mad effort to cash in on your dream. I have seen this happen too many times on *Shark Tank* when someone reveals that he or she has spent hundreds of thousands of dollars—sometimes even a million dollars or more—on a business venture that has gone nowhere and cannot be expected to succeed. When these dreamers have mortgaged their homes to continue pursuing a lost cause, it becomes tragic. I'm all in favour of success; I am deeply opposed to tragedy.

The risk must always be calculated and constantly reassessed. It's far better to admit failure and descend back to earth, perhaps to plot a new path to the top, than to remain frozen halfway up the mountain where nothing is achieved. In business, when assessing the risk against the reward, you always need to consider how and when to cut your losses if necessary; it's called an "exit strategy." When climbing mountains, if you stay halfway to the top, refuse to try for the summit and are unable to find your way back to the ground again, it's called "fatal."

Risk is a part of success—a big part. Whenever someone tells me he or she wants to achieve exceptional success without taking substantial risks, I know the person is not serious about reaching his or her goal. Because if you really don't want to do something, any excuse works.

The careful calculation of risk

Here are five ways to deal with risk by calculating it before you start climbing your mountain:

1. Measure your tolerance for risk. Some of the most successful entrepreneurs in history were content to constantly live on the edge where financial security was concerned, fighting off creditors with one hand while pulling themselves and their company to new heights with the other. In contrast, many business people prefer a more methodical approach, acknowledging the inherent risk but moving slowly and steadily. The degree of risk you should assume is the one that enables you to continue climbing without stress, unhappiness or sleepless nights.

2. Determine the probability of failure. When someone says "You can't lose!" (or when you tell yourself "I can't lose!"), you take the first step toward losing by believing this. The fact is, you *can* lose. Acknowledge that fact and grow comfortable with it. Take time to measure the downside of your risk and your comfort level against the possible loss. Taking a risk does not mean pursuing something that has a foolishly low chance of success. Taking risks in business is not like standing on the edge of a cliff and choosing to simply jump off into the water. Never jump until you've seen for yourself just how deep the water is.

3. Remember that risks are seldom fixed. Large companies reduce their risk level as a matter of routine by sharing both the risk and the profits, if it benefits them. For example, the producer of a commodity such as gold or wheat may negotiate a fixed price over a period of time, or may negotiate a volume of product with a buyer who wants to avoid price volatility. The price of the commodity may rise during the term of the agreement, costing the producer potential profit, but the benefit of guaranteed sales offsets the paper loss. Anything that is not firmly fixed, including risk, can be adjusted. Perhaps you can find a similar way of sharing both the risk and the reward in order to move closer to your goal.

4. Talk to people in the know. It's always nice to chat with friends about your venture, but accurately evaluating risks requires the opinion of experts. Before putting a major portion of your assets on the line, discuss your plan with an accountant, lawyer, banker or business advisor. Expect to pay a fee (negotiate before beginning), and give the advice a good deal of thought before proceeding.

5. Never ignore the wisdom of your instincts. After absorbing all the reflection, wisdom and advice available, pay attention to one more source of opinion: your gut. This is a difficult call, but the number of times that a great success has been built primarily on the instinct of its creator are too many to ignore. Example: nobody believed Fred Smith when he suggested a guaranteed overnight continent-wide delivery system, but he went ahead and founded Federal Express anyway. And few believed that millions of families would trek to central Florida, far from the state's celebrated beaches, for a vacation, but it didn't prevent the launch of Disney World. Both decisions were based on gut instinct, and both were loaded with equal prospects for success and failure.

24

What All Salespeople Should Know

Selling is probably my most important talent, and natural sales ability is among the first qualities I look for in a new employee. Anyone who can create or modify a program, and sell me or someone else on the program's superiority over its competitor's, is a winner in my book. I suspect every manager and entrepreneur shares the same attitude because they know and agree with the old maxim "Nothing happens until somebody sells something."

One area in which I differ from many company CEOs is managing salespeople. Some of the differences in my methods are due to my industry, and some are due to my unique approach. The differences encompass two areas: dealing with customers, and dealing with the salesperson's own company.

You can't sell today's buyers with yesterday's techniques

Traditional sales techniques have become so refined and codified over the years that they are almost like a memory test. Learn the key steps, deal with objections, listen for closing opportunities and—wow!—you're a champion salesperson!

These steps don't work anymore, and I doubt that they ever worked as well as some companies that made millions by developing and marketing sales courses back in the 1970s and 1980s claimed they did. Thanks to changes in society and the marketplace, buyers recognize that the balance of power has shifted toward them. A few minutes spent at their computers enable them to do their own research on features, benefits, pricing and even markup on items ranging from clothes to cars. They know a good deal about the product, pricing, options, configurations, specifications and competitors long before speaking to a salesperson. So they can tell when a sales pitch is stretching the truth. In fact, they almost expect that it will.

> " Thanks to changes in society and the marketplace, buyers recognize that the balance of power has shifted toward them. "

Buyers are far too sophisticated these days to act like robots each time a salesperson pushes this or that button. They are no longer programmed to buy; if anything, they are now programmed to resist manipulation by salespeople who continue to follow some supposedly "can't miss" sequence of questions and suggestions from a sales manual.

Too many traditional sales techniques are based on manipulation, and no one appreciates being manipulated. My approach to sales remains focused on meeting customer needs, but it involves far more than selling by rote. I believe in creating satisfaction first and making sales later. Like this:

Ditch the sales pitch and start a conversation. Instead of making a mini-presentation about themselves, their product and their company, successful modern salespeople need to learn about their customers. Buying decisions are based as much on rapport with the salesperson as on expected benefits from the product or service—maybe more. The more complex, expensive and vital the purchase, the more important the rapport.

Recognize that the first "good fit" has to be with the customer. Customers sense when salespeople are moving the discussion forward and preparing to close the sale. If no strong relationship exists between them and the salesperson, the customer's natural inclination is to resist. But when rapport has been established and their needs are being met in a convincing and beneficial manner, buyers begin to pull the salesperson into the purchasing process.

Establish trust. Most lost sales occur at the beginning, not the end, of the sales encounter. Traditional sales language is built around opening lines such as "I have a solution that is ideal for meeting all your needs!" or "Other companies just like yours are using this product and love it!" Sure, the lines may be benefit-oriented and express the salesperson's confidence. But they immediately define the roles: aggressive salesperson and potential buyer. On its own, this is a self-defeating strategy. Along with rapport, one of the first things that needs to be established between buyer and seller is *trust*. Like it or not, many potential customers simply don't trust salespeople—at least, not at the outset. Immediately defining the two

> " One of the first things that needs to be established between buyer and seller is *trust*. "

traditional roles, instead of letting them develop naturally, does not engender trust.

And, finally, here is a point I made in my previous book that deserves repeating: *Customers will always remember how they felt during your sales presentation long after they have forgotten the features you told them about.* Having fun in a sales meeting is always more important than applying sales pressure.

Meanwhile, back at the office

In review meetings with sales staff, I ask each salesperson to answer a series of questions based on his or her understanding of our needs as a company. I do this not in private meetings but in open sessions, with other sales staff present. It's not my intention to embarrass anyone. I just want to emphasize the importance of the facts. The questions include:

What is the gross margin our company earns on each of the primary products or services you sell? Sales representatives need to know more than the price the customer pays and the commission the salesperson earns. The third dimension to the picture is the amount of money applied to supporting the company. And if it varies from the salesperson's perception, why?

What are the relative volumes of each product or service on the sales list? How do they compare with volume? No one expects every sales representative to match the sales volume, by product, of every other salesperson on staff. But wide variations in sales volume may reveal an important situation, especially when lined up against the appropriate gross margin earned.

How closely do your guesstimates of these figures match the reality? This is the real eye-opener for both sides. If a sales representative's concept of gross margins, product volume and relative sales by category is substantially off target, what does it say about his or her knowledge of the true situation, including reachable sales quotas and other concerns?

For far too long, the flow of information, where salespeople are concerned, has been in one direction: from management to sales staff, shaped as techniques to follow and quotas to achieve. I believe we are now in an era when questions are just as important as directions—when management's knowledge of the underlying qualities of its sales staff is as important as the sales staff's knowledge of the products and services they are assigned to sell each working day.

25

It's a Sales Call, Not a First Date

The biggest challenge many salespeople face is the same one they couldn't handle when they were teenagers: rejection. To them, asking for the order is reminiscent of being back in high school and asking someone for a date, or hoping to be asked. Obviously, teenage trauma can stay with us to middle age and beyond.

Not for all of us. I remember hearing about a Hollywood film director who was casting for a major motion picture back in the 1960s. Many actors who knew about the movie wanted to be in it, including a young Robert Redford. When Redford approached the director and asked to be considered for the role of leading man, the director told the strikingly handsome actor that he wasn't suited for the role.

"Why not?" Redford demanded. "Tell me why I'm not right for the part."

"Okay," the director said. "What did it feel like when a girl turned you down for a date in high school?"

Redford looked confused. "I was never turned down for a date in high school," he answered.

"Precisely," the director said, and the conversation was over. The director was Mike Nichols and the movie was *The Graduate,* for which Nichols cast a more ordinary-looking and frequently dateless Dustin Hoffman. Hoffman's career was launched, *The Graduate* became a classic and Redford went on to other projects where the character's rejection was not a factor.

Get over the fear of hearing the word "no"

Hearing the word "no" is never fun, but in sales you're not exactly inviting someone to go to the junior prom with you. You're seeking a business deal that you fully expect will benefit both sides. Saying "yes" isn't an expression of approval of *you*; it's an approval of the deal you're offering and the way you're offering it.

I recall one of our salesmen asking for permission to offer a hefty discount and other incentives to a prospective customer. When I checked the original proposal I could see that it was well priced, on target and fair in its terms. When I asked if the customer had requested the discount, the salesman said no, she hadn't. "Then why build it in?" I inquired. The salesman replied, "I just wanted to make it easier for her to say 'yes.'"

Nobody enjoys hearing "no" in any situation, whether social or business. We are all programmed to seek approval for every request we make. For most of us, the deepest and most painful memories of being told "no" are from our adolescence, a period of life when we feel awkward because we don't fit in, and we are unsure of our place in the world. No matter how often we hear about others being rejected in a social context, it's painful when it occurs to us, and we never forget it.

But this wasn't a high school date. It was an opportunity to close a major deal for a highly sophisticated program to serve a crucial function on behalf of an international client—and it was being delayed by the salesperson's fear of rejection.

Anyone in sales who is too sensitive to deal with a negative response or so unrealistic that they believe every sales call must be 100 percent successful is in the wrong job. Stuff happens. To everyone. In every company. Deal with it.

Being overly sensitive to rejection can become a destructive virus. I'm all in favour of doing whatever it takes to make a successful sale, but not when it means going against the company's sales strategy or breaking its conditions. Being more concerned about avoiding "no" than achieving "yes" is basically bad selling.

> "Being overly sensitive to rejection can become a destructive virus."

Good salespeople do not assume that every failed sales call signifies personal rejection. Whenever a sales pitch isn't successful, they review their presentation and ask themselves if they did everything in their power to make it a success. If they didn't, they make a note to do things differently next time. And if they did their best, their attitude is to forget the missed sale, say "Next!" and move on to another opportunity. The last thing they want to do is dwell on the situation. As one salesperson put it, when it comes to not making a sale, "I have a memory like a goldfish."

Many things make a good salesperson, but I'm certain that the one quality common among all the top salespeople in any industry is a perpetually positive state of mind, one that easily dismisses a sales call that didn't bear fruit because they are convinced that the next pitch will be a brilliant success.

How salespeople can handle rejection

Here are the three things I tell salespeople to help them overcome the trauma of their sales pitch being rejected:

Acknowledge that you are permitted to undergo rejection now and then. A periodic lost sale does not mean you are ineffective. It may even be therapeutic if it discourages potential arrogance and encourages you to sharpen your sales techniques.

See the bright side to a customer saying "no." The customer's sales resistance has been dissipated, so he or she no longer feels pressure to make a deal. This can make that customer more receptive to the next sales presentation you make.

Never reject a customer when he or she turns down your sales pitch. Keep the conversation going, perhaps by promoting your company's new products and achievements. Besides helping to build relationships, this will establish you as something of an authority in your field, strengthening your hand for the next sales presentation you make.

Of all people, baseball legend Babe Ruth may be the best example of how to deal with an unsuccessful sales presentation. Most people know that Ruth held the record for the most home runs in major-league baseball. Many also know that he once held the record for the most strikeouts in a single season. During his career, Ruth knocked 714 balls out of the park. He also struck out 1,330 times, or nearly twice as often as he scored a home run. One day after a game in which Ruth had struck out three times in a row, a reporter asked him if he was discouraged. "Are you kidding?" Ruth supposedly replied. "Every strike brings me closer to the next home run." It's a point of view that works as well for salespeople as it does for sports heroes.

26

Why You Shouldn't Be Selling Salt

Most successful companies sell a combination of products and services. Your car needs repairing? You take it to someone who has the parts and the knowledge to fix it, and you pay for both. You need a special roast for Sunday dinner? A butcher chooses and prepares a cut, and both the meat and the butcher's skill are covered in the price.

Almost everything we purchase has both product and service built into the price, and it reflects the value of both. The more complex the product, the higher the price you can expect to pay for the related service. It doesn't take a lot of skill to pump your car full of gas. It does take quite a bit of skill to repair the transmission.

Unless they are engaged in a short-term strategic marketing ploy such as sampling, no business people I know give their product away for free. Yet many of them offer their services gratis as a means of closing a deal or winning favour with a customer, or in a desperate attempt to move product out the door. Under these terms, customers pay for the product but not for the effort to select, prepare and install it.

I have a problem with the concept of offering free service. My company was built on the superior quality of the services we provide. Nothing comes "off the shelf" at the Herjavec Group. Every client's needs are determined and measured before any solution is offered, and every solution comes with an installation schedule and sometimes training for the customer's staff. The service aspect of a sale makes a major difference to the customer's ultimate satisfaction and is a key factor in our company's steady growth in sales volume, in our client list and in the recognition we have built within our industry.

Customers don't resent appropriate charges for exceptional service, although I can understand that they would prefer not to pay them. They don't resent the charges because *they understand the value of the services we provide,* not just the price that we charge. If none of our services carried a price tag, we would be saying, in effect, that the time, skills and expertise of our employees are worthless. The same message would be passed along to customers if we hid the service charges within the price of the product we provide, a tactic often employed in our industry. You can't fool customers in that manner today. Why hide from customers what they already know they are paying for necessary service? Maximum transparency is best because it builds trust and loyalty.

" **Maximum transparency is best because it builds trust and loyalty.** "

Start by defining your company's value proposition

It's fairly easy to define your company's market and prime customer profile. It's even easier to identify your major competitors and their strengths and weaknesses. But what about your firm's value proposition—the aspect of your business that will swing prospective customers to choose you (you hope) over the other guys? The overriding quality in this instance is the value that customers assign to your company versus that of the others in the same business. The greater the perceived value—note that I say "value," not "price"— the more favourably customers will look at your company and the more likely they will be to give you their business.

If the core of your value proposition is the extent and quality of the services you provide, discounting or bundling these services tells customers that your services are worthless. Does this mean you should refuse to accommodate customers when they make reasonable requests during negotiations? Not necessarily. At our company we ensure that customers are familiar with the value of our services. Nothing is totally free; everything has a price, and somewhere in the equation, someone has to deal with the real cost. Here's an example:

> " Nothing is totally free; everything has a price, and somewhere in the equation, someone has to deal with the real cost. "

Some time ago, a client asked me to speak at a major conference his firm was hosting on the other side of the country. No fee was discussed; my appearance would be a goodwill gesture to make the customer look good. I agreed to address the session, but only after I instructed the sales representative to inform the customer that when I appear at speaking engagements (I no longer do paid public speaking except on rare and very special occasions), I am represented by the leading speakers' agency. I also noted that my normal rate for such an appearance was at the top end of the fee schedule. I had no intention of charging the customer the amount quoted by the speakers' agency; I simply wanted the client to know the *value* of the service I would be providing.

Offering complex services free of charge is more than bad business, in my opinion. It is an insult to your customers' intelligence and credibility. Buyers are far more aware of business operations now than they were just a few years ago. They are also, I believe, more suspicious about unexpected gifts and benefits from the firms they deal with.

Here's another aspect of customer behaviour you should know: customers tend to pigeonhole suppliers. It doesn't mean they are lazy or difficult. It just confirms that they are human. We all categorize people and companies into various groups according to our needs and perceptions. The pigeonhole you do not want your customers to slot you into is the one that identifies you as someone whose product is purchased strictly according to price, with no support offered or expected after the sale is made and the goods are delivered. When this happens to you and your firm, you become sellers of salt.

Salt is the ultimate commodity. You can dig it out of the ground or you can boil a vat of seawater until the liquid evaporates, leaving salt behind. The differences between one kind of salt and another are relatively minor, and most kinds of salt are indiscernible from one another where taste is concerned.

Like all commodities, the only real significant difference from the point of view of a buyer is price. If I can sell you my salt for 10 cents a kilogram less than the next guy, you would be foolish to buy the other brand of salt, even if the difference in price is so small. And if a third party comes along to undercut my salt by the same amount, how do I defend myself and my company and not lose profit? I can't. That's the nature of commodities.

> **Everyone in business needs to clearly define his or her value proposition and insist that customers remain aware of it.**

Everyone in business needs to clearly define his or her value proposition and insist that customers remain aware of it. It is essential to differentiate yourself from competitors, justify the price you ask your customers to pay and create customer loyalty. In my view, it remains as important as any other management decision you will make.

Unless, of course, your business is selling salt.

27

"Let's Wait and See What Happens," Said the Captain of the *Titanic*

Every industry faces challenges of one kind or another, and when the challenges aren't met or addressed, the impact shows up in lower sales.

I've made my career in computer technology, which continues to develop at a pace unmatched by any other industry in history. It's been barely 35 years since the introduction of personal computers. If the aircraft industry had advanced as quickly as computers and the Internet over the same time period, 35 years after the Wright brothers we would have been riding in supersonic pressurized aircraft capable of flying non-stop around the world. And here, depending on your point of view, is either the inspiring or the scary part about the speed of the technology: it shows no signs of slowing down—if anything, it keeps accelerating.

The speed of the industry's development brings good news and bad news with it. The good news is that technological developments mean our customers face new needs and new challenges, and they call on us to assist them. The bad news is that some-one can come from out of nowhere and pass us before we're fully aware of their existence. That's one cause of a drop-off in sales, but there are others.

Falling sales, or a sales volume that appears stuck on a plateau, can't be ignored. Economists define a recession as two consecutive quarters of economic decline. I would define a sales volume crisis as two consecutive months of declining sales. When a serious sales slump occurs, some sales managers and CEOs keep on plodding at the same pace with the same strategies, usually offering the sooth-ing suggestion that everyone should wait and see what happens.

I don't believe in waiting and seeing what happens. I believe in *making* things happen, and nothing spurs me in that direction faster than falling or even plateaued sales. Slimmer margins can be fixed and high costs can be lowered, but falling sales mean declining market share, and without sales there is nothing. My response to lower sales volumes is similar to that of a captain of a vessel that meets an unexpected iceberg: all hands on deck, sound the fire alarm and stand by while I get busy. "Busy" in this case means launching a three-staged response:

> "I don't believe in waiting and seeing what happens. I believe in *making* things happen."

Stage 1: I analyze the data and determine what it says. Sales figures can tell you a lot, but only if they are accurate and verifi-able. Data doesn't lie, assuming it is accurate and timely. Bad data leads to bad decisions. When I'm looking at sales figures and esti-mates, I want proof that the figures are accurate before I'll even begin to interpret their meaning.

Stage 2: I visit customers myself. Every step away from the real situation creates a filter, and when I'm looking for the cause of lower sales, I want the unvarnished truth. My staff will give me the facts, I'm sure, but I want to hear them as directly as possible. It's a matter of seeking total clarity. In film (remember film?), each copy away from the original photograph is called a generation. The sharpest, clearest picture you get with film-based photography is the first generation, and each generation away from the original picture grows a little fuzzier than the previous version. I don't want fuzzy; I want sharp.

I take the same approach when I meet with customers, asking why their purchases from us are down. I need answers to primary questions such as: What is the problem? Is it us? Are we not providing the product, the service or the value expected? Or does the problem originate with our customers? Is there a new decision maker who doesn't know us? Identifying the problem often is the first step toward turning things around.

Stage 3: I take a macro view of things. If our sales are declining parallel to a decline of sales within the industry, that's understandable and puts our situation in perspective. But if the industry is doing well and our sales aren't, the situation is more critical and deep-rooted. If your industry is growing by 20 percent annually, you need to grow by 21 percent just to keep pace.

New views on old-fashioned selling

I am often surprised and impressed by the way good salespeople find new ways of examining their profession and better ways of making it more effective. In our field, where the biggest risk to our customers is the one we don't yet know exists, expectations change as fast as the technology itself, creating a ripple effect that extends through the selling process. That's why we employ sales techniques that enable us to keep pace with developments in the industry.

Here are a handful of fresh approaches to selling that I have encountered. Good salespeople will grasp the advantages of these approaches and take them to heart, whatever product or service they're selling.

Forget sales messages; deliver buying messages. As long as the salesperson is seeing things from his or her perspective—that is, how do I get to closing a sale with this customer?—the picture will remain clouded. Buying messages are far more productive than selling messages. A buying message consists of information related to reasons the customer wants to buy your product or service. It has nothing to do with canned sales presentations and old fashioned "always be closing" techniques. Determine the buying message by identifying why the customer wants your product—that's the message you need to deliver.

Don't ask the customer questions you can answer yourself. I hate laziness. And I especially hate it when salespeople start asking me questions such as how many offices we have and what services we provide, when it's all on our website. If they can't bother to learn basic information about our company, how much effort will they put into working for me?

In the age of the Internet, basic questions can be answered even before you schedule the sales call, so why waste the customer's time asking about things such as product line, annual sales, personnel organization, branch offices and so on? Ensure you have this information in hand *before* making the sales call. Then you can invest time in engaging the customer and creating rapport.

Focus on value, not price. I've seen research that indicates price plays a role in buying decisions only about 30 percent of the time. More important than price to your customer is the value that will be delivered. With an appropriate understanding of value, price is rarely an issue.

I know a client who bought $4 million of a certain technology. After negotiating the lowest price available, she demanded an even lower price and gave up service to get it. She got the product at the price she wanted to pay, but could not get the technology to work. Two years later, most of the stuff was still in boxes, and the people who made the original buying decision were fired.

On a personal level, when my pilot tells me we need a certain part for my airplane and that we should buy it from a certain source because it offers the best quality, I don't ask if we can get it for 10 percent less somewhere else. When my family and I are on board the plane at 10,000 metres, I would take little comfort in saving 10 percent as we begin an emergency descent because the part failed. The value of having technology work well always outweighs its price.

Pleasure is an easier sell than pain. Some salespeople focus their efforts on the pain and problems of potential customers, assuming that customers will view them like the cavalry in old western movies, riding over the horizon with guns blazing just in time to rescue them. Or maybe they believe misery loves company.

But misery isn't fun, whether it's yours or someone else's. Move away from problems as quickly as possible and settle on solutions offered by the product or service being sold. And try to have some fun doing it.

This concept of pleasure versus pain can affect marketing and promotion decisions in ways that may not occur to you right away. Kevin Harrington, one of the original Sharks, is widely known as the Infomercial King. Kevin has sold hundreds of millions of dollars of products through TV infomercials. Once, when we were considering investing in a combination of a smoke and CO_2 detector, I suggested promoting it with a TV infomercial. Kevin advised me against it. According to Kevin, products based on fear of a house fire or CO_2 poisoning do not do well as infomercials because they appeal to reason. "People want pleasure when watching television," he explained. "Their reaction to a sales pitch for a product like that would be, 'It'll never happen to me.'"

Meet the right person at the right level. Sometimes the biggest mistake of a sales pitch occurs when the meeting is first arranged—with someone other than the decision maker. It doesn't make sense to schedule a sales pitch with someone who does not make decisions. You'll have to schedule a follow-up call with a superior, and going over your contact's head can create ill feelings that may jeopardize a good future working relationship. Generally, it's best to book a meeting with someone as high up the decision-making chain as possible.

Be aware that the higher you go on the organization chart, the more you have to sell value. The lower the customer is on the ladder, the more the discussion becomes about price. High-level executives are assigned to bring value to the business and take a longer view of performance and return on investment. Those on the lower rungs have a more myopic outlook.

Toss out trite selling techniques. I can't believe that someone who drives a brand-new car, carries the latest smartphone and has a wardrobe that showed in Paris just last week uses sales techniques dating back to the days of door-to-door vacuum cleaner salesmen. But it happens, usually with sales representatives who fail to meet their quota each month. The world is far too sophisticated for old ideas and more and more reliant on honesty and openness in business relationships.

To old-school sales types, some new ideas in selling sound like heresy. A generation ago, salesmen at the corporate level were advised to wear ties and dark suits as a means of making themselves look competent and ethical. Not today—or not always, at least. The important thing is to dress according to the situation. Make sure your appearance is suitable. You shouldn't dress over the top, as though you're on the red carpet at the Oscars, or look like you slept on the subway last night. You won't go wrong by matching your appearance to that of your client. Of course, once you're worth $2.5 billion, you can wear Skechers and a T-shirt to every meeting, like Mark Cuban does.

Get sharp instead of sloppy. Every word spoken to a prospect should be designed to strengthen the relationship and move toward a sale. I cringe whenever I hear a salesperson say to a new prospect, "Can I give you a call sometime?" That's sloppy talk and sloppy selling. Sharpen the words and the message. Say, "I'll contact you soon, and before I do you might think about this," following with some new or provocative sales point. Another sloppy line that has been touted for years without any sales payback is "What can I do to win your business?" Get specific, as in: "Do you have any potential objections about today's meeting?"

I hate it when a salesperson returns from a call and tells me that the man or woman they met is "really nice." I don't care about that. My usual response is to ask if we take orders only from "nice" people. Nice has nothing to do with it. Give me facts about the customer's business, expectations and needs, and the things required to make a sale. Deliver me from "nice."

It's not just about the questions you ask. It's also about how you ask them. Most salespeople know the questions they need to ask. That's the easy part. The magic comes from asking those questions without making the client feel that he or she just went through an interrogation. Getting the information you need without someone feeling as though you are grilling them is easier if you have a natural curiosity about people and the things they do. Curious people generally make great salespeople.

Never assume that you are smarter than your customer. Because when it comes to knowing what is needed, knowing how to measure value and knowing all the reasons to make the investment you are asking them to make . . . you are not.

28

Speak Less and Lie Never

Life is motion. You're always either staking out a position or moving to a new place that promises more opportunity and reward. When your life involves being responsible for a corporation that hundreds of people depend on for their livelihood, as well as for your own family—as mine does—the pace grows faster. Add in a number of pursuits that propel me into the public eye, such as my appearances on *Shark Tank*, and things really speed up. Whatever I say or do today I had better be prepared to defend tomorrow because someone, somewhere, will call me on it.

Most of the people I deal with are honest and would never consider telling an outright lie. I respect them for that, and I assume I have earned their respect through my own honesty. Truthfulness, after all, should be the norm, not the exception.

> " Life is motion. You're always either staking out a position or moving to a new place that promises more opportunity and reward."

Unfortunately, this is not always the case. *People lie to me all the time.*

The lies I hear as a businessman are not always defined as such, especially by the people telling them. And they rarely begin as falsehoods. They begin when people try to support weak facts with extended hope. A prospective customer's request for a "possible review" may evolve first into "a future sales presentation date," according to a member of our sales staff, and later to "a sure chance for a major sale." Similar fibs are passed along by customers and prospective buyers who don't want to give me bad news, so they postpone revealing that our competition has an inside edge on a sale through a lower price, more features or some other claim.

Good salespeople want to be friends with their customers, and great salespeople know there is a line they won't cross. In our ultra-competitive world, I want both good news and bad news immediately. I can't compete if I don't know the facts. But being friends with your customers creates a problem. No one wants to deliver bad news to their friends, so they tend to delay passing it on. When this happens, an opportunity is often lost or a bad situation is made worse.

We encounter a lot of truth-stretching on *Shark Tank*. Once again, they're not outright lies as much as facts supported by hope. Someone looking for an investment may claim to have sales of "almost $100,000" when they really mean something closer to $50,000. We have encountered situations where the pitcher for a deal neglected to mention that he or she did not own the patent on a key feature of the product, or that there was another major partner in the business. These may not be outright lies, but they are at the very least sins of omission. Does telling such tales destroy the chance of doing a deal? Sometimes, and sometimes not.

One example of stretching the truth as a means of supporting his hopes came from one good ol' boy from the southern United States, called Travis. Travis appeared on *Shark Tank* seeking an investment in a device he created to help people learn to play music. I liked the prospects for his product. More than that, I liked Travis, even though it's difficult to imagine two guys with more contrasting backgrounds than us. Travis's family goes back several generations in America's Deep South, while I'm a first-generation Canadian, born in Croatia and living in Toronto. Our origins may be a lot different, but one thing we have in common is a passion to succeed. Travis is passionate about his product. I have a weakness for people like that, and I believed in Travis 100 percent. He had overcome skepticism, limited capital and a lack of business experience to create, manufacture and market a product with unique qualities and broad market appeal. He's also a builder, like me. I love to build things, to take ideas and turn them into reality, just as Travis did. He is my kind of guy.

He is also a nice guy. Don't believe that stuff about nice guys finishing last. You need more than a nice disposition to be successful, but when you're pleasant to others, they usually respond by giving you a chance to succeed.

I recognized the potential of his invention; millions of people, young and old, dream of playing music, not necessarily to become famous but to relax, amuse themselves and perhaps entertain friends. But learning to play any instrument takes a lot of time, effort and dedication. Travis's product promised to help novice musicians start making something besides noise sooner than regular music lessons would. All five Sharks saw the market appeal and were impressed by Travis's personality. We were even more impressed by his success to that point. When I asked Travis his annual sales volume for his device, he replied, "Oh, 'bout half a million dollars," adding that he expected a purchase order to arrive shortly for thousands more units.

That clinched the deal for me. If Travis could do that much business on his own, the $125,000 investment he was seeking plus the marketing assistance I could offer him made this the best opportunity I had seen on the show in three seasons.

Things are always competitive on *Shark Tank,* but when we see a clear opportunity to hit a "ten-banger"—meaning a chance to earn profits of 10 times our investment—it can become very cutthroat. Whenever you hear the offers from the Sharks become more generous and our voices more strident, you know we have uncovered a potential gold mine.

Despite the competition, I managed to outbid the other Sharks to become Travis's partner and make both of us a lot of money while turning thousands of people into musicians.

It's established that every Shark agreeing to a deal will perform due diligence, checking the claims made by the people pitching the investment opportunity. When my accountants began to conduct due diligence on Travis's company, they were unable to confirm Travis's claim of a half million dollars in annual sales. The best they could estimate was a tenth that amount.

I still liked Travis and I liked the prospects for his product. I didn't like, however, being given a sales figure that was clearly overstated, and I called Travis to hear his explanation.

"Aw, hell, Robert," Travis said when I informed him of the problem. "Did I really say a half million? Shucks, what I meant to say was that I'd have a half million once the show's on TV." Like all reality shows, *Shark Tank* is recorded months in advance of its air date. Travis suspected, with some justification, that demonstrating his product to a national audience via the airing of the *Shark Tank* episode would boost his sales. Still, overstating his annual sales by a factor of 10 was too much for me to swallow, and I told him I was backing out of the deal.

Travis was persistent. He kept coming back to me, telling me he would easily do the sales volume he predicted, and asking that I reconsider my decision. Maybe it was because I was still impressed with the sales potential of his invention, or maybe it was because I liked Travis and his positive attitude, but I realized that he had no malicious intent in inflating his numbers. Yes, he had stretched the truth, but the product still had all the promise I had recognized before I heard Travis's sales figures.

I decided to work with Travis, making a suggestion here, adding a new idea there, and watched as sales started to climb. Then, on February 3, 2012, the episode of *Shark Tank* with Travis's presentation aired, and almost overnight his sales figure estimate was no longer a bullish estimate; it was a confirmed prediction. The day after the show appeared, orders began flooding in. Travis's product was going to be as big as I had suspected and as Travis had predicted.

Before that *Shark Tank* episode aired, Travis was selling three units and generating about $100 in sales each day. Six months later, annual sales were approaching $2 million and the company employed 20 people full time. That's the power of a good idea, a great product and national television exposure.

Even though his *Shark Tank* appearance provided a boost big enough to make my investment less critical to his success, Travis didn't ask to renegotiate his deal with me. Some *Shark Tank* participants have pleaded for an investment during their presentation, expressing great joy and gratitude when they get it. Later, when their earnings begin to grow, the same people begin insisting on renegotiating the terms with their *Shark Tank* partners, squeezing more profit out of the investor's pockets and into their own. Travis didn't do that.

The sales volume for his product traced a classic parabolic arc, rising higher week by week. That's the good news. The bad news is that every arc has a downside, and soon we will have saturated the market. By then we'll need another related product to replace the initial sales wave and enable us to scale the company up to a larger sales volume and a broader base. How? Stay tuned.

Good communication involves speaking—or not

As a business leader, your communications with employees can serve to build their trust in you and in one another. Some of my ideas may seem counterintuitive, but if you give some thought to the impact that acting upon them could have on the people who matter, I suspect the advice will begin to make sense. Where possible, communicate directly, that is, by speaking, rather than writing, to employees. Or, as you will see, by not speaking at all.

Remember: the goal is to build respect and trust in you and in the values of the company, not to build your own ego.

Three ways good leaders handle communication

Actions, as we know, speak louder than words. So when words are needed to communicate with employees, good leaders give as much thought to how and by whom the words will be spoken as to the words themselves. Here's how:

Avoid being the person to deliver good news. Unless you are the only one involved in whatever good development has occurred, choose a subordinate who contributed to the event to make the announcement and share the glory. You will bolster that employee's confidence, increase his or her trust in you, and demonstrate to everyone in your organization that you value and respect that person's contributions.

Always be the person to deliver bad news. Even when the failure or the decision had nothing to do with you directly, don't shovel the bad news onto someone else's shoulders. As a manager and a leader, it's the only honest way to deal with bad news. Being honest isn't easy because it makes us feel vulnerable. As much as the truth can hurt, and as uncomfortable as it may make you feel, you cannot be totally honest if you avoid the issue. Honesty is not a task to be checked off a to-do list every day; it's an ongoing process. Being prepared to handle the dark days as well as the sunny ones comes with the job of being

> **"The goal is to build respect and trust in you and in the values of the company, not to build your own ego."**

leader and personifying the company. To your employees, to your staff, to your suppliers and to your customers, you are the company, and you cannot build trust in the company by shrugging off the tough jobs.

Don't speak when there is no news. Some leaders and managers think meetings are like rainy days—if you don't have one once in a while, something is wrong. "I know there isn't much to talk about," they may say when everyone has gathered, "but I thought getting together might be a good idea anyway." No, it is not. It is a waste of time and effort.

29

Pamper Your Strengths and Play Down Your Weaknesses

Anybody reading the sports pages or following NFL football in early 2012 heard all about quarterback Peyton Manning and his search for a new job.

Manning was 36 years old, which, for a player in the NFL, is ancient. He had spent his entire professional sports career— 14 seasons—with the Indianapolis Colts, who released him in March 2012 after he suffered a neck injury late in the 2010 season.

Throughout his career, Manning never kicked the ball, rarely blocked an opposition player and carried the ball an average of just 50 yards per season. Yet when he left the Colts, the only NFL team he had known, in search of a team with which he could play until he was 40, almost every team in the league was eager to sign him. He chose the Denver Broncos, which offered a contract worth $100 million, a figure he may double through endorsements and other income sources.

Think of it: $100 million for a football player who neither

kicks, blocks nor runs with the football. Why would anyone pay that much?

Because Manning can pass the football perhaps better than anyone in the game. For six consecutive seasons he threw the football for more yards to score more touchdowns than anyone else. Proving that when you can do just one thing well enough and often enough, little else matters. It's all about knowing your strength and building on it. That's what makes winners.

> " When you can do just one thing well enough and often enough, little else matters. "

Manning illustrates another quality common to all winners: they don't whine; they work. He had been the "franchise player" in Indianapolis for his entire professional career, leading the team to two Super Bowls and 10 consecutive winning seasons, and being chosen the NFL's Most Valuable Player four times. Then, after one bad season, two bouts of surgery on his neck, and the Colts' acquisition of a younger quarterback at a much cheaper price, Manning was released. He signed with the Denver Broncos and may yet lead them to the heights he achieved with Indianapolis, but he made the move without complaint. He knuckled down and did the job, and that's why he will always be a winner.

Always deal from strength

Strength can be found in various places in your business. The most commonly applied strength is the one built on the skills and experience you have acquired over the years. Don't consider these the only sources of strength, though. In business, the only tactic that counts is the one that wins within legal and moral boundaries. You apply whatever strengths you have to cross the line ahead of others, and sometimes this has nothing to do with cold hard logic and everything to do with relationships.

Recently, the Herjavec Group was pitching for a major account with a large prospective client. We were more than in the running for the contract; we had the product, the application, the service and probably a price advantage, although this last aspect was less of a factor than the others. We were selling Internet security, after all, and the most critical element of the job was ensuring to the greatest possible degree that the customer's data and transactions would remain safe.

Everything came down to a decision between our firm and our biggest, most aggressive competitor. The competition had a more dominant name, substantial clout based on its size, and a generally larger footprint in the market, which defined its strength. By other measures, it would be practically a toss-up. At times like these, the slightest nudge, the smallest positive difference, can swing a buying decision one way or the other.

One of the perks that the other guys offered was their powerful branding, the kind that only a multibillion-dollar company can afford. When we took the prospect to a hockey game, I realized that the entire arena was sponsored by our competitor. We couldn't win this fight. The other guys would always be able to offer access to most sporting events and have better tickets. So we would have to change the battlefield, and we did.

That year I began racing in the Ferrari Challenge series, which included an event at the Toronto Indy. The Challenge series is open exclusively to owner-drivers and racing professionals, which means amateurs like me are pitted against seasoned veterans, including the winner of a Daytona 24-hour race.

I would be racing my Ferrari 458 through the summer, including an appearance at the Toronto Indy in early July. When the Indy people learned I would be competing while their event was taking place, they offered to pay me to help promote the race: a Dragon/Shark tearing around the track at 300 kilometres per hour was sure to attract some media coverage. I told them I would be pleased to promote the Indy, but instead of paying me in cash, they could reimburse me by letting me have the track to myself for an hour each day.

When they agreed, I had the opportunity to drive clients around a live racetrack at 250 kilometres per hour, with 100,000 people watching from the stands. Spending $20 million to sponsor a hockey game is impressive, but not many companies can offer their clients a ride in a Ferrari race car.

I told our sales team, "Spending two or three hours watching some guys skate around chasing a puck is appealing, I guess. But I'll bet spending two or three minutes in a Ferrari race car travelling 250 kilometres per hour with a Dragon/Shark at the wheel is cooler." You can't sit around and moan about the advantages that your competitors have. You need to be creative, build on your strengths, discover a way to outflank the other guys and get it done.

Building strengths versus battling weaknesses

Digging for your strengths may be a little more difficult than inviting customers to share your corporate perks or strapping them into a race car. The important message is to identify your strengths, especially in contrast with your competition's, and apply them—something not enough businesses do. Why not? Because they are too busy addressing their perceived weaknesses.

I came across some research measuring the approach of businesses in various countries when it came to dealing with strengths and weaknesses. In the United States, about 45 percent of the efforts of top managers and corporations generally focused on developing strengths, with the remaining 55 percent targeted to fixing weaknesses.

I understand the approach—no CEO or manager feels good about admitting his or her weaknesses, either at an individual or a corporate level. Things are very different in China, where 73 percent of companies polled said they were focusing on developing their strengths. This makes sense to me—focusing on and developing your strengths helps you to win, because *you gain a much bigger advantage over your competition when you heighten the impact of your strengths rather than reduce losses due to your weaknesses.*

" Strengths can be developed to an almost limitless extent; weaknesses can be resolved only to a fixed degree."

Look at that statement a little more closely, inject a shot of basic psychology and it all begins to make sense: strengths can be developed to an almost limitless extent; weaknesses can be resolved only to a fixed degree. Think back to Peyton Manning:

In football, runners are generally of two types—power runners with lots of body weight who generate momentum either to push tacklers out of the way or run over them, and lightweight sprinters whose speed and manoeuverability enable them to outrun or otherwise evade tacklers. Both get the job done, but in different ways. If you lack either physique, you will never compete with the specialists. Manning is neither a bull nor a sprinter. He does not run with power or with great speed, and while he may improve his running ability marginally, nothing can change those cold hard facts.

But two out of every three times Manning threw the football during his first 14 years as a professional, somebody on his team caught it. Imagine focusing all of his effort on improving that figure by about 10 percent, from a completion rate of 66.5 percent to one of 75 percent. Instead of completing two out of three passes, he would be completing three out of four. Wouldn't this be far more productive than trying to become a better runner?

This isn't to suggest that weaknesses can be ignored, especially if they are enough to cripple an individual's or a company's total performance. But this is not about ignoring weaknesses; it's about ensuring the best allocation of resources. The first priority should be to bring your strengths up to as near optimal performance as realistically possible. Then you can pay attention to solving or at least minimizing the negative impact of your weaknesses.

Working with your strengths makes you feel good, and feeling good about your job is a major plus. Think back to your school years. If you enjoyed math but hated writing essays, which homework assignment would you turn to first? I'll bet you felt better about yourself when you tackled your math homework and then moved on to the essay with more confidence and momentum.

Now put yourself in your employees' shoes. They will be far more motivated and engaged when you encourage them to develop their strengths than when you insist that they work on their weaknesses.

The idea of stressing strengths over weaknesses is catching on in business. Unfortunately for American companies, it appears that the strategy is more popular in China than in the United States. In a speech made at the British Benchmark for Business conference in September 2010, Marcus Buckingham reported on a Gallup research project in which U.S. and Chinese business people were asked if it is better to focus attention on strengths or on weaknesses. According to Buckingham, only 41 percent of Americans polled said that attention should be paid to strengths over weaknesses. Compare that with the 73 percent of the Chinese companies choosing that strategy.

> "Your employees will be far more motivated and engaged when you encourage them to develop their strengths than when you insist that they work on their weaknesses."

Buckingham also noted that another study found that just 14 percent of employees played to their strengths during the average working day. That's an enormous waste of time and talent. In those companies, 86 percent of potential productivity was being wasted because people were spending the equivalent of that much time on tasks that they were less qualified to perform well.

Here's another thought: most employee weaknesses are an extension or a reflection of the individual's personality. Good writers tend to be introspective, even withdrawn; good salespeople are outgoing and comfortable in many social situations. Does it really make sense to try turning a shy writer into a two-fisted salesperson? Would it help your sales staff if they became as adept at drafting and polishing their sales reports as qualified writers?

I know a professional golfer who has tremendous power and great accuracy driving the ball off the tee, and exceptional putting skill as well. But his ability to chip a ball out of the bunker is abysmal. How does he spend most of his practice time? Driving off the tee and putting on the green. Why? Because he knows he'll perform these actions on every hole he plays, but he may land in a bunker perhaps once each round. Can you see the wisdom of his decision?

Good managers acknowledge the strengths of their employees, and they ensure that they have all the opportunity they can handle to perform according to those strengths.

There are always ways to deal with weaknesses. Start with automation and delegation. Can you obtain a computer program that will handle some elements that you, your staff or your company generally are weak at performing? Better still, can you comfortably move a job responsibility from someone who struggles with the work over to someone else who has a flair for the same task?

Prepare yourself for the kick that comes with working from your strength. Working from strength banishes concerns simply by providing you with the opportunity to do things you enjoy with the likely prospect of success. This in turn encourages the limbic system of your brain, its pleasure centre. When it's stimulated, you feel good about your work, your life and yourself.

I can't think of a better working environment for anyone.

30

Problems Are Problems First and Opportunities Later

I agree with those who say that we often learn more from our failures than from our successes. But problems are not always opportunities, at least not at first. They're difficulties, setbacks, glitches, obstacles and a dozen other things.

The idea that every problem is an opportunity has become a squishy kind of mantra cited by people who believe that all business and personal goals are within the reach of anyone if only you put your mind in the right place, maintain a healthy outlook and maybe eat lots of granola.

"Everything I am and have achieved is the product of effort and optimism."

I'm in favour of developing and maintaining a positive attitude. As I have said over and over in books and speeches, everything I am and have achieved is the product of effort and optimism. I believe in all the wise things written about modern management and business practices, including those I mention in this

220

book. But I also believe, just as deeply and just as passionately, in choosing reality over platitudes.

No one was ever asked to solve a mathematics opportunity

When your schoolteacher handed you a math project to solve, was it called an "opportunity"? I doubt it. It was properly labelled a math problem, and you treated it that way—a situation demanding a solution, a solution that could be reached only by applying knowledge and effort. The same definition applies in life and in business.

Suppose a friend owns a chain of franchised restaurants netting him a million dollars a year in income, and he offers to sell them to you. They are well located and well managed, and as long as people keep eating food, the restaurants are likely to keep producing healthy profits. A million dollars a year in net income—hey, this is an opportunity, right? No, it's a problem—your friend wants $20 million for the chain and you barely have cab fare to get home. That's the difference between an opportunity and a problem.

When the energy giant Enbridge had a major pipeline spill in Michigan in the summer of 2010, 3 million litres of oil spilled into the Kalamazoo River running through a wildlife refuge. To make things worse, heavy rains the following day caused the river to overflow banks and dams, spreading the oil over dozens of square kilometres of rich farmland and recreational areas. Soon video footage and photos of birds and amphibious creatures covered in thick black oil were being flashed across airwaves and on newspaper pages. Americans who had never heard of Enbridge before the spill began associating the company name with disaster and risk. Michigan residents gathered in town halls to condemn Enbridge and demand that the company not only restore the land to its original condition and pay for damages caused by the leak but also ensure that such an event never happened again. Two years later, the cleanup was still going on.

To the company's credit, Enbridge responded quickly and effectually, but the price was enormous no matter how you measure it. Enbridge estimates its out-of-pocket costs at $725 million, and it's clear that the incident soured much of the United States on construction of the TransCanada pipeline the following year. This might have been an opportunity to test Enbridge's response to a crisis of this sort, but beyond that, it was an enormous problem. You can categorize it as a failure of sort, with a lesson attached. Claiming it represented an opportunity is ridiculous.

I'm not suggesting you will always avoid problems, or that you won't be able to turn some problems into opportunities, which I have managed to do from time to time. I'm proposing that the first step you need to take is to solve the darn problem, *then* look for any opportunities.

You need problem-solving talents, not opportunity exploitation

Labelling every problem as an opportunity is wrong because it creates an unproductive mindset. Serious problems are not serious opportunities—they are crucial situations that must be dealt with and solved. Looking at them as opportunities can lead to errors, including a tendency to underestimate the gravity of the situation and the implications of not dealing with it quickly and adequately. Your most important need in the middle of a crisis is a raft of problem-solving skills, not opportunity-exploiting abilities. When you examine the problem in this manner, you will be provoked to muster all the available resources to deal with it—and that's what you should be doing, instead of congratulating yourself because another opportunity has popped up. A hole in the bottom of your boat is a problem; fix it before you sink.

Maybe it's true that you will look back when the problem has been solved and recognize some benefit that evolved from it. But you might have reaped the benefit without the problem if you had been more alert. Is waiting for a crisis to develop the only way to improve things?

When encountering a barrier, a failure, an unexpected development or anything that appears to stand between me and success, I don't assume a Pollyanna attitude, defining the problem as an opportunity. It is not. It is something to be dealt with quickly and smoothly because time spent on solving problems is time lost in realizing my goal.

> "Time spent on solving problems is time lost in realizing my goal."

Many problems can't be solved by me alone. Various groups and individuals within the organization often need to be aware of a problem and committed to solving it. Frequently, the biggest challenge is drawing attention to the seriousness of the situation.

I have a technique for doing this: I make people uncomfortable.

If you're physically comfortable, things that would normally concern you are easy to ignore. That's the reason people go on vacation; whether you're lying on a beach, climbing a mountain or pedalling across Europe, you're enjoying yourself too much to apply your mind to sales drop-offs, margin shrinkage or a recurring customer complaint. You have to get back from vacation, physically and mentally, before you're able to deal with those problems.

Often, however, the people I need to deal with the problem are just down the hall, not relaxing on a beach somewhere. Their minds may or may not be on vacation, but I know I will need 100 percent of their attention to recognize the seriousness of the problem and begin dealing with it. I do this by disturbing their comfort zone.

There's nothing like calling an early-morning meeting to focus everyone's attention on a serious problem. I'm talking seven in the morning or even earlier. If this happens on a cold, dark winter day, the impact is even greater. Staff may not be pleased about rising earlier than usual and filling themselves with coffee to keep alert, but they will quickly absorb the situation and the steps needed to get past it.

Besides rattling people's comfort level, these meetings impose a gentle discipline on everyone involved. Breaking the normal routine to arrive at the office at an unusual hour and leap directly into problem-solving mode imposes order on all employees. I'm no fan of tight regulation and ordering everyone to fall into line, but I have no doubt that one of the most important qualities an army needs to achieve victory is internal discipline, something that has worked since the time of the Romans. Everyone at the

Herjavec Group possesses internal discipline, although every now and then some nudging is needed to rouse the collective synapses to deal with a critical problem.

No one at my company ever confuses a problem with an opportunity. Problems can lead to opportunities, just as getting lost in a jungle can lead to an unexpected discovery. But at the outset, only one fact remains: problems are problems, and they deserve attention, not applause.

31

Failure Can Be Good Training for Success

Unsolved problems have their consequences, and often the consequences involve failure—failure to secure a key contract, failure to meet sales or profit goals, failure to succeed at the endeavour you chose.

I've already said that every failure is a lesson, and that I place more value on a person who has dealt with failure, and admitted it, than on someone who claims never to have encountered it. The former is wiser than the latter, and the latter either cannot be trusted or has never set substantial personal targets .

For ambitious people, success is merely a moment in time, an event that, once achieved, fades away. Failure, or the risk of it, is a full-time companion for entrepreneurs. And while failure brings lessons, they're obviously worth avoiding if possible. There are ways to avoid failure, or at least reduce its frequency somewhat. After all, if the price of the lesson is higher than you can afford, you are no further ahead.

This is a variation on the old maxim that "experience is the best teacher." It may be so, but sometimes the teacher can exact a price that is much too high. Someone once used that expression when discussing the importance of experience with Marshall McLuhan. McLuhan said he could just imagine a condemned prisoner being led to the gallows, thinking, "Well, this will teach me a lesson."

Don't fail at learning from failure

It's easy to say you will learn something from a failure, but it's more difficult to determine just what you will learn and how you can make the lesson work for you. This becomes a serious challenge when the failure is organizational rather than individual or systemic.

It's too easy, for example, to be superficial about the cause of failure by saying, "Procedures weren't followed." That's like saying an aircraft crashed because the pilot didn't land it correctly— there has to be more to the story. Sometimes the answer is more like an excuse than an explanation, as in "The market wasn't ready for our product." The market will no doubt apologize for its role in your failure.

It seems to me that the most important thing to do in assessing a failure in an organization is to place more emphasis on the cause and less on the blame. There is a difference, after all, and it's worth remembering. "Engineering didn't understand the scope of the problem when they designed the program" clearly blames one department. "We

> " The most important thing to do in assessing a failure in an organization is to place more emphasis on the cause and less on the blame. "

were unable to communicate all the parameters of the project when we established the objectives" is likely more accurate and far more helpful, I suspect.

Failures are not always disasters, but they're never much fun, either. While it's not practical to plan on being successful 100 percent of the time, it's certainly worthwhile to plan on avoiding failures in the first place. Failures that don't kill you are worth the lesson, and any failure that doesn't cost you money is a blessing in disguise.

Ten ways to sidestep failure

1. Have a clear sense of purpose. Average people have no clear purpose in life, which is why they remain average. Reaching levels of success that are well above average demands setting purposes for your life, your job and your week. Weekly purposes are goals you want to achieve in the next seven days, and should be limited to one or two.

2. Steer clear of destructive thinking. Avoid smothering your ideas and those of the people around you by always assuming the worst. In addition to letting you give in easily whenever confronted by a challenge, it could damage your mental and physical health.

3. Ask the right questions. The right questions tend to be big ones, with universal applications. Examples: What do I stand for? What does my company stand for? What do I expect of myself and my staff? What could go wrong with this new idea, and what can I do to prevent it?

4. Value EQ more than IQ. Most of life doesn't concern the things that happen to us; it concerns the way we *respond* to the things that happen to us. In times of stress, our emotional quotient is more valuable than our intelligence quotient. People with a great ability to find the square root of anything won't prove nearly as impressive if they cannot think straight under pressure.

5. Avoid building your life around money alone. This may surprise some people, but the most important things in my life do not include the money I have made. They include my family, my relationships with friends and colleagues, and the contributions I can make to both my business and my community. Money won't keep you warm at night or give you a sense of purpose, and if money is your only measure of success, you will always fail because somebody, somewhere, will always have more—more money, more cars, a bigger jet, a larger yacht and on and on. I started my first business to make money, but I have since learned (and I wish I had learned sooner) that real greatness doesn't come from the pursuit of wealth but from having a true purpose in your life—one that is bigger than yourself and is not measured in money.

6. Always focus on your strengths. Everyone is more familiar with his or her weaknesses than with the strengths they possess. Think of your strengths as a mass of muscle. The more you exercise this mass, the stronger and more efficient the muscles become.

> " Think of your strengths as a mass of muscle. The more you exercise this mass, the stronger and more efficient the muscles become."

7. Sometimes thinking is more important than doing. Successful people are always busy, but the most successful of them are often busy thinking rather than doing. Find time to reflect on ideas, suggestions and objectives.

8. Feed your self-image daily. A good self-image, free of arrogance and conceit, helps you face every day and every problem with confidence. Don't let a success blow your self-image out of proportion, and don't let a failure weaken it.

9. Consider ideas as gold and persistence as platinum. The most common cause of failure is giving up too soon. The difference between success and failure is often just one more try.

10. Build a wide and solid network. Nobody in business achieves total success on his or her own. We all depend on a network of people—suppliers, clients, staff and personal supporters—to help us reach our goal.

32

A Club of Takers

My goal was always to achieve success in business. It took some time to determine what that business might be, but when I recognized just how much impact the computer revolution was going to make on the world, and all the opportunities it would present to an entrepreneur, I knew I wanted to be part of it.

I never planned to become part of the celebrity circuit, however.

The upside of being a celebrity: a daughter's happiness

I enjoy the perks of fame that my television appearances have brought me. I don't grumble about not being able to go somewhere without someone recognizing me and asking for my autograph, or wanting to discuss a recent TV episode. You can't have it both ways; you can't revel in the glamour and glory one day and grumble about losing your privacy the next. You need to find a method of dealing with celebrity or walk away from it entirely.

The most enjoyable part of my celebrity status is not the good feeling I get from it but the ways I can use it to make others feel good, especially my family. Here's an example.

One Direction is the biggest boy-band phenomenon since the Beatles. Hundreds (maybe thousands) of girls my daughter Skye's age lined up for days just to catch a glimpse of the singers. When One Direction arrived in town in early 2012, a colleague at CBC invited me to meet them. Naturally, I asked Skye to come along. Skye and I were ushered past the waiting fans into the TV studio, where the band members were preparing for an interview. We weren't going to just catch a glimpse of these newest teenage heartthrobs; we were going to be introduced to them and talk with them.

Is this kind of special treatment fair to people without fame and connections? Probably not, but it exists and has always existed down through history. The opportunity for my daughter, as I saw it, may have been granted to her because she was my child, but it had been earned by me through years of hard work and dedication. Who would I be hurting if I refused the invitation? Myself? Not really. The girls who had stood in line for hours? Again, no. But by accepting the invitation I would be making my daughter happy, however briefly, so I agreed to go.

We were walking toward the band's dressing room when the door opened and Harry, the lead singer, stepped into the hallway. Looking our way, he stopped in his tracks, his jaw dropped and he said in a classic British accent, "Oh my god—it's the man from *Shark Tank*! Can I have my picture taken with you?"

My 15-year-old daughter, who is usually very conservative and controlled, was awestruck. Later, after we had met all the boys in the band, she began sobbing uncontrollably, and I grew concerned. When I asked what was the matter, she said, "I am so happy that I can't stop crying."

Do you think a father enjoys making his daughter so happy? This one does, immensely. And could it have happened unless her father had enough celebrity status to obtain the invitation? Not a chance.

A stranger in a somewhat strange land

Since I never harboured any dreams of becoming a celebrity—which I hasten to add is a term others hang on me; I never hang it on myself—I am fascinated by the whole process. What is there about being seen regularly in a network television show that changes someone in the eyes of a large segment of the population? The achievements I have made as a businessman were much more demanding, in my opinion, than sitting on a platform with four other successful businesspeople, listening to an aspiring entrepreneur make a pitch for money.

> " People have become more interested in every aspect of celebrities' lives, and it's something of a double-edged sword. "

The difference is television, and I understand that. I do my work behind closed doors, but I listen to business pitches in millions of living rooms. People recognize my face, my voice and my name. This type of recognition has been happening to TV personalities and actors since families first gathered around the

TV set. Things have changed, however. People have become more interested in every aspect of celebrities' lives, and it's something of a double-edged sword. Of course, it's fun to be recognized and have strangers approach you with smiles and compliments. It also raises concerns. Somebody said, "The last remaining luxury in life is privacy," and I buy that completely. The reason that interest in the stars is greater than ever, I suppose, is the Internet, which brings celebrities and their fans together easily and more closely.

The Internet is changing society so quickly and so completely in this fashion that people who study these things (generally known as social scientists) measure fans' interest according to something they call the Celebrity Attitude Scale.* This fascination with celebrities seems to be like caffeine—it's healthy up to a point. It's a means of social bonding, escapism and entertainment. It's probably also another one of those behavioural habits handed down from cave-dwelling ancestors who needed to know as much about strangers as possible because they were more likely to stick a spear in you than neighbours. I'm not sure how that translates into a fascination with Jennifer Lopez's butt or Justin Bieber's hairstyle, but otherwise it seems to make sense to me.

I've been caught in the middle of this because I can be as starstruck as anyone. It all depends on the star. And I see it from the other side when I am approached by fans of *Dragons' Den* or

---

* L.E. McCutcheon, R. Lange, and J. Houran, "Conceptualization and Measurement of Celebrity Worship," *British Journal of Psychology* 93 (2002): 67–87.

Shark Tank who ask for my autograph and become as awestruck as I was when I first met Oprah Winfrey and Celine Dion.

The whole celebrity world is a strange land in many ways. I enjoy visiting it, but I am always relieved when I return to my home, my family and my business. Things are more real there.

Fame is no prerequisite for business success

I appreciate all the by-products of fame that are available to me, but I avoid getting wrapped up in them. It's not as difficult as you may think.

You can't avoid fame when you are in the entertainment business, and if that's your life's work, you had better learn not just to accept it but to relish it. People like George Clooney and Meryl Streep are famous because they are stars, and they are stars because they are famous. The two roles are impossible to separate, whether George and Mcryl like it or not. Take away their fame and you take away much of their identity.

In business, many successful and respected people have little or no fame beyond their industry, and they take pains to keep it that way. They don't need to be part of a celebrity circuit to achieve everything they want. In fact, fame is often more of a hindrance than a help to them. Corporate lawyers may want everyone in their business to know what they do and how well they do it, but they're rarely interested in achieving similar recognition elsewhere.

I actually quit *Dragons' Den* after the first season. I enjoyed it and the experience was interesting, but I decided I'd had enough of it. Of all people, it was Kevin O'Leary who talked me into coming back. Because he likes me? Maybe. The main reason, however, was that he knew we brought a certain chemistry to the show. He wasn't doing it for my sake (but I will always be grateful to him for it). He was doing it for the good of the show. In typical Kevin fashion, he said, "You're an idiot for quitting! This show is going to be huge, and you'll become a big celebrity and it will benefit your business!"

He was right, to a degree. We sell to large enterprises, not mass consumers. A consumer-oriented brand whose spokesperson or CEO is a TV star enjoys a huge advantage over its competitors. Kevin has proved it with the success of his O'Leary Funds and, most recently, his O'Leary line of wines. In my case, my TV presence was a deterrent in the beginning. Competitors would say to our clients, "Are you going to deal with some guy on a television show? Is that how serious you really are about your security?" Only when the show became big did my celebrity status really help the business. Having people know about you before you walk into a room is a benefit, especially when you're competing against huge companies.

Some business leaders actually seek fame beyond their own fields. Jack Welch wanted to become a celebrity as much as any Hollywood star after retiring as CEO of GE, and Warren Buffett's name is familiar to millions of people who have never invested a penny according to his financial guidelines. Steve Jobs, I suppose, was the ultimate business celebrity, although he avoided media appearances except when launching a new Apple product.

So it's easy for me to keep my acquired fame in perspective. Being a celebrity is not my business, and aside from the kinds of perks I enjoy from time to time and can share with my family, it makes little impact on my life.

Rating celebrities from A to D

Because my primary interest is in business rather than television exposure, I look at the celebrity scene with a cooler eye than others. The whole celebrity milieu is in many ways a large club of takers. Members of the club can be fun to be around, generous with their time and effusive in their praise. I don't doubt their sincerity for the most part, but I keep my eyes open and my expectations lowered.

The most important thing that most celebrities value in people they first meet is any opportunity for the person to advance their career. You can be charming, brilliant, successful and fashion-model attractive, but unless you can add to the celebrity's success, the encounter is likely to be fleeting. When you're hot, everyone loves you. When you cool down, nobody cares. I've been to parties where I was the biggest celebrity in the room until a bigger name showed up. Then I was just another guy standing on the sidelines.

The industry rates fame in the usual manner: A, B, C, D, and so on. The Brad Pitts and Oprah Winfreys of the world are obvious A-level celebrities, and the industry determines the other levels to the point where most know just where they stand in the rankings. One of the saddest sights I have encountered is the sudden deflated ego of a C-level celebrity when an A-level star enters the room. Suddenly all the people who were hanging on every word of the

C-level celebrity, rushing to bring refreshments to her, begin treating her like a piece of furniture, pouring their awestruck attention onto the bigger name, the brighter star, the A-list celebrity. Whenever I witness this side of celebrity life, I am grateful that I have a fascinating, challenging and successful business to run.

> **"It takes risk and drive to achieve celebrity, but when you reach the top, what do you have?"**

I have often stressed the risky aspect of being an entrepreneur and the drive it takes to build a business from nothing more than an idea into a substantial corporation employing hundreds of people. It takes risk and drive to achieve celebrity, but when you reach the top, what do you have? In many cases, a book of press clippings and the awareness that eventually your identity as a star will fade. That's when you become a has-been.

I don't resent people who are hungry for recognition. I have sampled it, and I have to admit that it's enticing. When you reach a certain level of fame, doors that were once closed suddenly open for you, and things you might never see or experience at any price fall into your lap for free. For a while, your ego shines as large and as brightly as the sun. Here's the difference: You can count on the sun shining forever. Being a celebrity? Not nearly so long.

I don't dislike the celebrities I have met in recent years. In fact, I respect almost all of them. But I admire them for the things they have achieved, not for the fame that hangs on them like a robe. You can learn a good deal from an individual's achievements. I'm not sure what you can learn from counting how often their photo appears in *People* magazine.

33

What's Going On Outside the Office Window?

I am grateful that I live in a country with a free, democratic government and a tradition of tolerance.

My parents didn't enjoy true freedom until they emigrated to Canada from Croatia because my father insisted on speaking out against the Communist system that dominated the country. After being arrested and jailed numerous times for daring to criticize the government, he was warned that if he was convicted again he would be shipped to a prison on the Yugoslavian version of Devil's Island and probably never be seen again.

No one was going to tell my dad that he couldn't speak his mind, so he chose freedom for himself and his family. None of us ever regretted the move, despite the years my father then spent sweeping floors in a factory, which was all the work he could find in a country where he didn't speak the language.

Freedom and democracy brought my father the right to criticize and demonstrate against government policies, a right that he craved to exercise back in Croatia. Knowing my family's experience, this right to free expression is an entitlement I will always treasure. No one should ever take that right for granted.

> " This right to free expression is an entitlement I will always treasure. No one should ever take that right for granted. "

So I may have been a little more tolerant than others of demonstrations by the Occupy movement that swept across much of the world in 2011 and 2012. The Occupy demonstrators aimed their wrath at the "one percenters," the minority who control much of the wealth in nations, often at the expense of the 99 percent of people with far fewer assets. I have not performed the calculations, but I suspect that I fall within the "one percenters" category. Do I resent or disagree with the protesters? No, I don't. Many of the practices and situations that outrage them affect me in similar ways.

I bear no guilt about the level of success I have achieved. Neither won in a lottery nor inherited from an ancestor, my assets were built up over many years through hard work and sacrifice by me and those around me, and we did it openly, fairly and legitimately.

Does wealth create motivation or resentment?

When I was a young man, access to the level of wealth that I enjoy today was a motivator, an inspiration for me to set my goals high, raise my energy level to the maximum and match the level of success of the person whose wealth I admired. Times have changed. Now, when people see that same level of wealth, it doesn't produce motivation. It produces resentment.

That's a dangerous development. Wealth gained by true entrepreneurs should be an incentive, an example of what it is possible
to achieve through imagination, dedication, hard work and, yes, a
little luck from time to time.

Builders always accumulate substantial amounts
of wealth. Along with their earnings, builders create jobs and material goods, including houses and
vehicles, that others can use in a practical manner.
Few people resent someone who earns money and
accumulates wealth by beginning with little more
than an idea and determination.

> " Wealth gained by true entrepreneurs should be an incentive. "

Dozens of examples exist of people who blended an idea with
a lot of energy to generate personal wealth. One of the best is Phil
Knight, who began selling athletic shoes out of the trunk of an
aging Plymouth. For a year or more he drove the car up and down
the Pacific coast of the United States, attending track meets, where
he would demonstrate his shoes, selling a few pairs here and there,
and sleeping in the car when he didn't make enough sales to pay for
a motel room. He believed in his concept of quality athletic shoes
at attractive prices, and that the appeal would spread from track-
and-field meets to the general public. For a brand name he chose
the Greek goddess of victory: Nike.

Over time, his Nike shoes launched an entire industry of
sophisticated athletic footwear. At last count, Knight's company
employed an estimated 200,000 people worldwide, and his personal net worth was in excess of $14 billion. He has donated hun-
dreds of millions of dollars to various charities and universities.

Knight *built* something to create his wealth. His energy and vision created jobs and tangible assets. Raw materials are prepared and purchased, products are designed and assembled, retail stores promote and sell them, and people around the world slip on Nike shoes to compete, to play or just to feel comfortable. Whatever you may think of one individual accruing that kind of wealth, you can't deny Knight's success at creating something that exists only through his vision and energy.

It may come as a surprise to some, but the motivation to build a business entity is not exclusively to become fabulously wealthy or even to earn a profit. In fact, profit is often seen as secondary to the satisfaction of creating something that once existed only in the builder's imagination. You cannot dismiss the power of a vision to drive entrepreneurs and build wealth. Not for me. Not for anyone.

> " You cannot dismiss the power of a vision to drive entrepreneurs and build wealth. "

Creating something out of dreams

On the Ferrari Challenge circuit, I race against Damon and Ryan Ockey, two brothers who have built a home construction company operating in Alberta and Florida. Relaxing between races one day, I asked the Ockeys about their business and the satisfaction it provided them.

"You know what the best thing is?" Damon said. "It's when we drive through a community, a whole neighbourhood of houses and parks, and we see people enjoying themselves and getting together. We see kids and dogs and barbecues and all of that, and we remember that just a few years ago this was just an empty field with nothing on it except weeds and rocks. Now it's a place for people to raise their kids and enjoy their lives. That's unbelievably satisfying." They built something out on the open land, and they took a lot of pride in their achievement. That's the motivator that true entrepreneurs understand.

When the Ockey brothers asked what was the best thing about being in the computer business, my answer was similar to theirs. "I walk through my office," I said, "and realize that nine years ago none of this existed. Not the offices, not the jobs, not all the activity of people being busy and making a living." I didn't launch my company so that I could afford to race cars. Racing just satisfies an itch. My ambition has always been to build a company—create an organization of substantial size and success and employing a lot of people who share my vision.

The Occupy movement did not and should not target people like the Ockey brothers or Phil Knight in its expression of outrage, and I suspect that most Occupy protesters don't. Their wrath is directed for the most part at the element of North American business who feel entitled to receive outrageous amounts of money for doing little more than moving paper from place to place. They're not builders. They're shufflers.

Kevin O'Leary and I differ in many ways, and one of them is the way we approach making money. I view money as a means of doing things I enjoy, while Kevin appears to see it as an end in itself. The profits my company earns enables me to continue building it. Along the way I expect to create opportunity and wealth for others. I don't believe Kevin sees money in the same fashion. I want to use it and he wants to accumulate it.

Kevin is hardly alone, and he's not even the worst of the breed. What of the business school graduate who walks into a $200,000-a-year income on Wall Street? Or the brokerage part- ners who demanded their annual million-dollar bonuses after their companies were saved from bankruptcy by an injection of taxpayers' money? Or corporate CEOs who dismiss thousands of employees because they have no other means of boosting the company's profits, then pocket severance packages totalling hundreds of millions of dollars when they leave their own jobs?

So I understand the resentment expressed by members of the Occupy movement. I also understand similar reactions from the general public. I agree with the reasons behind the protests and the anger. But not everyone with wealth above a certain level deserves to be dumped into the same bucket. I hope that the people who support protests against excesses like the ones I mention make a distinction between those who build an organization as a measure of their success and those who reap millions because it comes with their status and position.

It's the basic difference between Mark Cuban and Kevin O'Leary. Both are tough negotiators, hard-nosed businessmen and possessors of immense wealth. Cuban, for all of his edgy competitiveness, is a builder, a guy whose primary energy is directed toward creating an organization of people directing *their* energy toward a shared vision.

34

A Lesson from Oprah

My family and I have a vacation home on a private island in southern Florida. It's a popular escape location for many people, including various celebrities. Julia Roberts, Jim Carrey and tennis pros Andre Agassi and Boris Becker all have residences there. It's easy to see why. Along with the climate and access to nearby Miami, it provides privacy and a laidback lifestyle.

Given all the well-known people who live on the island, it's no surprise that they keep to themselves. It's a place, after all, to get away from hoopla and excitement. The island is less than a kilometre across at its widest point, and everyone either walks or rides in golf carts, which is appropriate because all the residences are located on the perimeter of a first-rate golf course.

The Florida climate that provides much of the island's appeal is as changeable there as anywhere in the state. One minute you're basking in a soft sunlit day, and the next minute you're in the middle of a drenching downpour.

That's exactly what happened one day several years ago.

Diane and I had recently purchased our home, and I decided to explore the island in my golf cart. When the rain arrived unexpectedly, I turned the cart around and headed back to the house, shielded from the water by the cart's roof.

Ahead of me I saw a woman who had apparently set out for a walk in the sunshine, unprepared for the rain. When I pulled up alongside her and asked if she would like a ride, she turned, smiled and said, "Oh, would I ever!" At the sight of her face, my mouth dropped open. Was this Oprah Winfrey? I was almost sure it was. Not 100 percent certain, but it sure looked and sounded like her.

This was honestly exciting for me. I have enormous respect for anyone who rises from nothing to achieve huge success, and no one personifies that achievement better than Oprah. But was this really her seated next to me in my golf cart? I couldn't let this moment pass without introducing myself and talking with her, but I was doggone if I was going to ask, "Say, are you Oprah Winfrey?"—which would have been very uncool.

Fortunately, Oprah had published an exercise and weight-loss book that I had recently read, so I said casually, "I just read your book, and I thought it was great. Really good stuff."*

I said this as a means of confirming that it really was Oprah Winfrey seated next to me. If it was, I expected her response would be "That's nice," or a simple "Thank you." Instead, her face brightened with that famous smile, and she looked at me

* Bob Greene and Oprah Winfrey, *Make the Connection: Ten Steps to a Better Body—and a Better Life* (New York: Hyperion, 1999).

and said excitedly, "Really? Thank you so much! Which part did you like best?"

Oprah was not only flattered to receive a compliment on her book from a total stranger; she wanted to know which part of the book I, the stranger, had enjoyed most.

I had finished reading the book just a few days earlier, so the material was still fresh in my mind. I mentioned the chapter in which she discusses training to run a marathon, and how, if you enjoy drinking red wine, you can't consume several glasses of it and hope to run the following day. It underlined the kind of commitment needed to even participate in an extended run, let alone hope to be a serious contender.

It turned out that Oprah's residence was almost next door to mine, so each time we encountered each other on the island, she greeted me with that billion-dollar smile, a big wave and a "Hello, Robert!" in a voice familiar to people around the world.

The gap between who you think celebrities are and who they really are

The lesson I learned from my encounter with Oprah was that, no matter who they are and whatever social standing they have, everyone appreciates being treated with respect. It's as if we all carry a sign around our necks that reads "Please be nice to me."

I have learned to speak to people on their own terms and to never assume that I know and understand every detail of someone's life just because his or her story has been spread across newspapers and talked about on television. I also realize that, as much as many celebrities have achieved, there may be a gap between who I think they are and who they actually are.

I was recently watching a rehearsal of a show starring Pitbull, one of the truly great entertainers to come out of the rap scene. He had attended a taping of *Shark Tank* and, after Daymond John introduced us, Pitbull invited me to check out the rehearsal for a show he was putting together.

Pitbull—his parents are from Cuba and his real name is Armando Christian Pérez—is a great-looking guy whose appearance, demeanour, wardrobe and voice are all packaged perfectly. The man was born to be a star. During the rehearsal I was seated near several show business executives, including the producer of the show being rehearsed. "Wow, I like this guy," I said to the producer. "He is so well-spoken and bright. Really impressive." A woman seated in the next row overheard what I had said and agreed with me. She was a senior executive with RCA's entertainment division and was familiar with many show business personalities. "I love Pitbull," she said. "He's fantastic!"

Hearing this, the producer smiled and replied, "You only love him because you spent a couple of hours talking to him." The RCA executive, a competent and hard-nosed businesswoman, had a point to make. "Exactly," she said. "He is the only artist I could stand talking to for that long."

She may have met, chatted and negotiated with dozens, even hundreds, of artists and performers over her career, but none was as capable as Pitbull of carrying on an interesting discussion with her. On stage, Pitbull can perform songs with titles like "Hotel Room Service," "Krazy," and "Give Me Everything." Offstage, the guy can talk about licensing agreements with a broadcasting executive or international economics with a business executive.

Pitbull adapts to the interests of corporations and individual business people. Although a lot of great artists are out there polishing their acts, assembling their backup groups and perfecting their performances, not all of them can do this. It's one reason Pitbull is, and likely will remain, a star.

> **"Talk to people in their own language. Understand their interests and their point of view, and tailor your words to suit them."**

Lesson learned: Talk to people in their own language. Understand their interests and their point of view, and tailor your words to suit them. And maybe, just maybe, with enough talent and a lot of hard work, you could be rapping or dancing or singing in front of millions. Or maybe achieving the success you've always craved in the business field. The lesson applies equally well to both scenarios.

The thing that most people get wrong about David Foster

While in Las Vegas, my wife, Diane, and I spent time with Celine Dion. Celine has so much talent and such a presence that it's difficult to get beyond the qualities that make her such a giant star. Being with Celine is almost like hanging out with royalty—neither Diane nor I know quite what to say at times.

We did, however, strike up a great conversation with David Foster, a giant in the recording industry and the guy responsible for so many of Celine's hit records. In addition to producing records for Celine, he was also the guiding force behind recordings for Michael Jackson, Mariah Carey, Whitney Houston, Beyoncé, Prince, Barbra Streisand, Andrea Bocelli, Toni Braxton and Madonna. Along the way he has won, at last count, 16 Grammys for his work and untold other awards.

"One good measure of success is how quickly you can recover from the inevitable mistakes you make."

David invited Diane and me to join him and some friends for dinner. During the meal we talked about the secret of achieving success in show business and in life generally. He's a bright, lively and energetic guy with lots of opinions, and we began discussing the true measure of success and how it is that, when you reach a certain level in almost anything you do, people think you're infallible. David clearly reached this level several years ago, but he is the first to admit that he is not infallible. And he has the stories to prove it.

During the discussion, he and I agreed that one good measure of success is how quickly you can recover from the inevitable mistakes you make. This led to talking about how so many people familiar with your work and achievements assume you have never made mistakes at all.

When people who meet David for the first time talk about his work, a lot of them mention the songs he did with Celine and how much they enjoy them. David then asks which of the songs is their favourite. Almost without a moment's hesitation, most people answer "My Heart Will Go On," from the movie *Titanic*. It makes him smile.

"Celine brought the song to me," David said, "and wanted me to produce it for her." But when David looked over the melody and the lyrics, he was not impressed, and he advised her against it. "If I were you," he told Celine, "I wouldn't do this song." Celine was disappointed, but she insisted on recording it, even after David dug in his heels and refused to be involved with it. You probably already know "My Heart Will Go On" won the Academy Award for Best Original Song and became not only the bestselling single of 1998 but one of the biggest-selling popular songs in history.

"And I have to tell all those people who believe I was the genius behind it," David said with a smile, "that of all the songs I produced with Celine, that one had nothing to do with me."

In the recording industry, most people believe that no one has a better ear for a pop song and a better sense of what makes a hit record than David Foster, and they're probably correct. But, as David said, his experience with "My Heart Will Go On" also proves that just when you think you have everything figured out . . . you probably don't.

How I really feel about show business

If anyone had suggested a few years ago that I would be riding in a golf cart with Oprah, dining in Vegas with Celine Dion or hearing recording-session secrets from David Foster, I would have laughed aloud. Me, hanging out with names like that? Hey, I'm a guy who works with computer nerds.

I enjoy the perks that have come my way thanks to my appearance on *Dragons' Den* and *Shark Tank*, but that aspect of my life has never defined me and never will. This may surprise some people. It even surprised my wife, Diane, and no one knows me better than she does.

In the summer of 2012, just before the taping of the very first episode of *Dragons' Den* in which I would be absent from the panel, Diane and I were invited to the launch party. It was great seeing everyone again and meeting David Chilton, who would fill the chair I had occupied for so many years. We had fun, and on the way home Diane asked me if I was disappointed about no longer being on the show.

"Not at all," I said. "I had fun and I liked everybody on the show, including the production people. But it's over, and I'm fine with that."

"That's because," she said, "you still have *Shark Tank*. But you'll be disappointed for sure when that show ends."

"Not a bit," I said.

"Why not?" Diane asked.

"Because," I said, "I would rather go to work than go to a TV studio."

And I meant it.

35

Short Careers and Long Traditions

One night Diane and I some had friends over for dinner, people who are hard workers but have little knowledge of various aspects of business.

Much of the talk at the time concerned the impending lockout between the National Hockey League and its players' association. Our friends were big fans of NHL hockey and decried the potential game stoppage while the players' association and the team owners wrangled over money.

"Those hockey players really have it made," one man commented. "Think of all the money they make just for playing a game. They should be ready to settle for less. Why, they're making more money in a season than anybody!"

"Anybody?" I replied. "Even CEOs of big companies?"

"Sure they are," he responded.

I suggested we do a little research on the subject, and we discovered that NHL players earned, on average, $2.3 million per season. That's a fair amount of money, but not really that impressive compared with the average $10.5 million paid to CEOs of Fortune 500 companies each year.

"Either way," the man replied, "a hockey player only needs 10 good years and he's set for life. After making $23 million, he can walk away from the game and retire, probably by age 30 or so. Wouldn't that be great?"

Reaching the peak of something you have worked for all your life and walking away from it would be unimaginable. I think that, along with talent, three other ingredients are essential to succeed in hockey or any other professional sport—a love for the game, total dedication and immense sacrifice.

Top-level athletes rarely sprout into greatness at age 20 or even age 16. Especially in hockey, they're identified as young as nine or 10, and much of their life from that point forward is groomed to carry them as far in the sport as their abilities can take them. Bobby Orr was first scouted as an NHL prospect by the Boston Bruins when he was just 12 years old, and Wayne Gretzky was attracting attention as an NHL prospect at an even younger age. Even for immensely gifted players like them, it took literally thousands of mornings, rising at 5 a.m. to practice or play prior to a full day of school, and spending their days and nights practising instead of attending parties and other social events with their peers, before an NHL career was possible.

If and when they finally reach the big time, earning a million dollars or more each year for playing a game and seeing their faces in the media day after day, is it really plausible that any of them would say after just 10 years, "Hey, I think I'll stop now and play a little golf for the rest of my life?" Not really.

It's never entirely about the money

Almost all the retired professional athletes I've met mourned the end of their careers in the sport, whether it was caused by age, injury or something else. They had a sense of loss that pained them deeply. Athletes spend a few years at the top and then they're told, for whatever reason, that it's all over. Even though they know from the beginning that their careers as players will be limited by age or injury, many have difficulty dealing with it when it happens. Each time I hear about a professional athlete choosing to retire at the top of his or her game, I question the truth of the story. Some players realize their best years are behind them and they can't compete at the same level any longer, and retirement becomes their only alternative. Other great athletes refuse to believe it, and they'll seek to join other teams in an effort to prove they still possess the drive and the physical ability to play one more season. Think of Brett Favre, Joe Montana, Roger Clemens and dozens of others. It doesn't matter how well-off they may be financially—they still want to get out on the field or the ice and feel the thrill that has driven them much of their lives.

Wanting to achieve greatness not for the monetary reward but for the love of what you do to earn that reward is not restricted to sports, or even to business. I remember reading about Gene Vincent, the early rock 'n' roll musician who toured the world and sold millions of records, only to discover as his career was winding down that his managers and record companies had basically stolen most of his earnings through bad deals and one-sided contracts. When the story broke, an interviewer asked Vincent if he was bitter to discover what he had lost.

"Not really," Vincent said.

The reporter was amazed. "Why not?" he asked. "These people got away with so much of your money."

Vincent smiled and replied, "But I had all the music."

I'm hardly suggesting that Vincent was pleased to learn how badly he had been treated by business associates he trusted. But it's clear that music, not money, was the thing that gave him so much satisfaction over the years.

The idea of an athlete choosing to walk away from the game at age 30 because he or she has managed to save and maybe invest a few million dollars during their playing years is inconceivable.

> **"There is always more to achieve— more markets to explore, more growth to plan, more targets to reach."**

Why? *Because it's never entirely about the money.* Mostly it's about their love for the sport, their competitive spirit, the camaraderie of their teammates and the recognition of the fans. If the sport is their life, what does it mean when their sports career has ended? The money they made can't replace it.

This is one reason I love business. At age 40, most professional athletes have reached the end of their careers; their best years are behind them. For most business people, age 40 is when they begin shifting into high gear. Whatever they may lack in energy they can more than make up for in wisdom, experience and networking. There is always more to achieve—more markets to explore, more growth to plan, more targets to reach.

36

The World Is Looking East

During our time, we are witnessing perhaps the biggest shift in economic and social power since Columbus returned to Europe to announce that he hadn't reached India but he might have "discovered" something better.

Western values and culture have dominated the world for 300 years or more, beginning with those of Britain and its various allies and enemies, and shifting through the last century to those of the United States. That's about to change.

I'm not going to join the legions of people declaring that the United States is slipping inevitably into disaster. The country has too much energy and assets for such a prediction to be valid. It also represents qualities that much of the rest of the world envies, including exceptional personal freedoms. But the growing power of China, India and other countries cannot be ignored. China drives the world's economy in

> "The growing power of China, India and other countries cannot be ignored."

many ways, including its use of natural resources, its manufacturing power and its ability to finance the debt of other countries around the world. That kind of influence is sure to be felt eventually in other areas, including culture.

This is hardly news to anyone even moderately aware of world development, but I think it needs stating in the face of changing attitudes in North America.

I'm sorry that the manufacturing sectors of Canada and the United States have declined to such an extent. It's a natural response to the fact that products from raw materials can be made at a fraction of the cost elsewhere in the world. Markets always react to better value, and while a country can use tariffs and customs duties in an attempt to protect one market from the influx of exports, in the long run it is an impractical option. History has proven that free markets work best.

> **History has proven that free markets work best.**

I write these words fully aware that manufacturing provided the bulk of well-paying jobs for people of my parents' generation. It was manufacturing that provided my father with the income he needed to feed his family while living in a society where he understood little of the customs and even less of the language.

I recalled that point during an episode of *Shark Tank* when a certain pitcher was demonstrating his product for us.

"And do you know what the best thing about my product is?" he asked. "It's the fact that it's made right here in America and not over there." Then, sweeping his arm in what I assumed was the general direction of China, he added, "By foreigners."

I find that kind of attitude deeply annoying. I'm sensitive to it because I am the child of immigrants—or "foreigners," as the guy making the pitch for our money put it. I recalled my father telling me that he often made suggestions at his workplace for small improvements that could make a major difference if implemented. In every case he was rebuffed, usually with a variation of the phrase, "What do you know? You weren't even born here." My father overcame this kind of insult, and the notion that only native-born Canadians were clever enough to have worthwhile ideas revealed not my father's weaknesses but the other guy's ignorance.

My response to the man who boasted that his product was made in America instead of "over there" was that I got his message. I knew what he was trying to say—"Made in America is good"—but every time I hear those words I hear nothing but bad. I hear closed minds, I hear protectionism, I hear an attitude that rejects the idea of anything new being introduced from "over there."

I'm perhaps sensitive to that kind of thinking because I spent too many years hearing people tell my father and me that we were not good enough because we had not been "made" in America or Canada. My view today is "Let the immigrants come in!" North America is still the land of opportunity, and the vast majority of immigrants arrive not only to pursue a dream but to work hard making it a reality. They're the kind of people who build great nations, and the more who arrive with that kind of ambition, the greater our country will become.

The message of China's preference for Buicks

The continued shift in manufacturing from North America to the east (India and China) and to the south (Brazil and other emerging countries in Latin America) is not going to be easy for us, and it's not going to be without pain and challenges. But the reality is, it's already happening and it cannot be halted.

A recent study indicated that China will soon have as many middle-class wage earners as the entire population of the United States. These Chinese will have every right to claim the same luxuries that middle-class North Americans have enjoyed for generations—comfortable homes, quality furniture and cars—lots of cars. Are we going to tell 300 million Chinese families that, due to limited oil reserves and concerns about global warming, they should not buy cars like the ones driven in Ontario and Ohio?

I was fascinated to learn that the most coveted new car among urban dwellers in China is a Buick. Does any car brand reflect more upwardly mobile middle-class aspirations than a Buick? The next generation of Chinese will carve out their tastes and adapt their culture to changing times and technology. And there is no doubt that China faces a number of challenges in its move toward widespread affluence. But the news that the Chinese are currently marking their upward growth in socio-economic status by aspiring to it in ways identical to North Americans was a revelation to me. In socio-economic terms, it is as though an entire generation of Chinese suddenly became 1980s-era North Americans, creating a new consumer-based economy almost overnight. What impact will China's move have on the future?

Protectionist policies and demands that everyone "buy American" or "buy Canadian" are not the solution to restoring the old state of affairs. The best long-term response to the situation is managed free trade and more open immigration.

Canada, of course, is already a nation of immigrants (as any First Nations member will confirm). The 2011 census revealed that two-thirds of the country's growth since 2006 was the direct result of immigration. Or, to put it another way, for every baby born in Canada during that period, two immigrants arrived to increase the country's population.* More than 6 million Canadians, or better than one in five of us, was born outside the country.

Since I'm one of those 6 million-plus, my opinion may be considered biased, but I honestly believe that Canada needs more immigrants, not fewer. The baby boomers born between 1946 and 1966 are withdrawing from the labour force in massive numbers, creating a double-blow impact on the country's economy: while paying far less into government coffers through income and other taxes, they will begin drawing far more from the country's treasury through sharply increased use of health care and social services.

Who will replace these retirees in the workplace? Not native-born Canadians—the birth rate of 1.5 children per family group isn't sufficient to maintain the numbers, let alone fill

---

* Richard Johnson, "Graphic: Where Are Canada's New Immigrants Settling? The Homelands & Homes of New Canadians," *National Post*, February 10, 2012, http://news.nationalpost.com/2012/02/10/census-canada-2011-where-are-canadas-immigrants-coming-from/.

the job vacancies. Immigrants who leave their home, their culture, their security and their identity in search of a better life in Canada will value those opportunities to work here.

Economists can dredge up dozens of reasons immigration will be the key to Canada's prosperity in the future, but there are other benefits to immigration besides economic ones. One of them is cultural. I believe that art, music, drama, cuisine and all the other elements that define a people and their nation become richer with new influences. Those who arrive here from Asia, Africa, the Caribbean—anywhere the culture contrasts with Canada's—will enrich the life we enjoy. They will also, I suspect, create a new Canadian culture that is unique— one that our grandchildren will treasure.

Stick around and see if I'm not correct.

37

It's Never about Where You Come From

In the spring of 2012, I visited Pier 21 in Halifax, Nova Scotia, where my parents and I landed in 1971 with one suitcase and 20 dollars.

I've told this story often because it measures many things. Among others, it measures the range of opportunity that Canada provides everyone who has an appreciation of its qualities and a will to win. I also stress that my story is not unique. Between 1928 and 1971, when Pier 21 closed, about 1 million immigrants to Canada passed through the same entry port as my family and I did. The year before I returned to Pier 21, I had been named one of the Top 25 Canadian Immigrants. Given my love for Canada and my success in this country, it was a great honour that provided me with a good deal of pride.

When I began studying the background of 2012's award winners, I was struck by how many other immigrants to Canada have come so far on their own terms, and how each story is both unique to each individual's background yet common as a measure of determination and success. The stories of these three Top 25 Canadians make my point.

Francis Atta arrived in Canada as a young boy from Ghana with his parents and 13 siblings. They settled in the Jane-Finch area of Toronto, one of the most troubled neighbourhoods in the city. Instead of succumbing to enormous peer pressure and giving in to the challenge of being an immigrant among so much social and economic strife, Francis graduated from college with a 3.87 GPA and launched several social programs to assist immigrant kids just like him.

Isabel Cisterna came to Canada from Chile unable to speak English, which naturally hampered her dreams of becoming an actor and a playwright. Even when she learned the language, her heavy accent prevented her from obtaining acting roles. She could have abandoned her dream, but she didn't. She became her own theatre producer. She launched a one-woman show that became a smash hit, followed it up with more productions and became a leader in local and regional arts movements. She also attracted attention in her home country, receiving an award from the Chilean government for her work in Canada.

And how would you feel about fleeing Vietnam to spend 12 years as a stateless person in a Philippine refugee camp, not arriving in Canada until you were in your mid-30s? Wouldn't you mourn that the best years of your life had been wasted, and decide you should just find a way to get by? Ai Thien Tran might have done this, but he chose instead to enrol in a social work program at McGill University, ultimately winning the international Golden Key Award for academic excellence and graduating with a 4.0 GPA.

Aside from performing other duties, he serves on the board of the Ottawa Parole Office. I like Tran's comment when he was asked how it felt to be named one of Canada's top 25 immigrants: "We've all been given a great opportunity here in North America. I'm not going to waste my chance or take it for granted."

A great beginning despite the scars

Most immigrants to Canada face similar challenges when they arrive—an inability to speak the language fluently, an unfamiliarity with social customs and values, and sometimes open hostility from native-born Canadians. The hostility can range from teasing to outright rejection, and even when you know it comes from a very few people who do not represent the vast majority of Canadians, it always leaves a scar or two. Many immigrants must still deal with some of these challenges.

More than 40 years after arriving in Canada, I still think that the day I walked through the doors of Pier 21 was a great beginning. I wouldn't change a thing about it.

Some scars remain from my early experiences, and if I try I can recall the angst I felt. But the memory of pain—both emotional and physical—eventually fades. I've often heard that if women remembered the pain of childbirth, no woman would have more than one child. I remember situations when I was teased, but I don't recall the pain I felt. More than that, I am always aware how far I have come, and it gives me enormous inner confidence.

It also stops me from judging recent immigrants I may encounter. Afghans, Pakistanis and Nigerians arriving in Canada today are the Croatians of a generation ago, and the Irish, Italians and Ukrainians of the generation before them. They land in Canada with little more than a dream of making a better life for themselves and their children, which is what my parents had. When I meet them, I never see their skin colour or hear their heavy accents. All I see is another immigrant with a dream, and all I hear is another mother and father trying to help their children.

When you have experienced the challenges faced by immigrants, it becomes very hard to judge others. My story of what I encountered at age eight is the same as the one being told by immigrants today. I've been there. I know what they are dealing with.

So looking around the restored Pier 21, now a national museum chronicling the immigrant experience, was humbling. Among other things, it reminded me of the sacrifices my parents made for me—first bringing me here and severing their connections with friends and family in Croatia, and later giving up many comforts in order to provide every opportunity they could for me. As I walked away from Pier 21, I asked myself a lot of questions. Did I do enough to show my gratitude to my parents? Did I give enough back to them? Was I kind enough to them? Was I as gentle and caring as I could have been?

" The length and difficulty of the journey we take are more important than the destination we reach. "

I am pleased that I visited Pier 21, and I believe that every Canadian, native-born or immigrant, should visit it and think about their roots. Some of us have journeys through life that are longer and more challenging than those of others, and immigrants to any land are quickly made aware of this. The length and difficulty of the journey we take are more important than the destination we reach, and they shape us in ways we may never fully understand. Indeed, the destination does not define us nearly as much as the effort we put into reaching it does. Destination, after all, is not identity.

I came across a saying recently that sums this up rather well:

What you've got is what you've got.
What you do with it is who you are.

38

Going Home and Growing Up

I spent the first eight years of my life living with an aunt and uncle in Zbjeg, a tiny rural village about 150 kilometres east of Zagreb, where my parents lived and worked. The house had a dirt floor and no plumbing, and there were more pigs, cows and chickens in the town than people. Each morning everyone headed for the barns or the fields to get their work done, and on most days the work continued til sundown.

It was a have-not kind of life, totally different in many ways to the lifestyle I encountered in Toronto. Looking back, however, I realize that I had acquired something in Zbjeg that I brought with me to Canada and that, in many ways, was responsible for who I have become and what I have achieved.

As you can tell from my description of Zbjeg, we had few material things to enjoy there. This was not as important to us as you might think. At the risk of sounding like a song by the Beatles, it is amazing what you can do in life when all you have is love. None of us had anything of real monetary value, but the people around me treated me as though I were the centre of the world. They would do whatever was necessary for my health and happiness, which gave me enormous confidence in myself. It wasn't arrogance—it's hard to be arrogant when you live in a house with a dirt floor and use an outdoor privy. Somehow I acquired confidence to attempt whatever I wanted to achieve in life because I knew that, no matter what happened, I would always be loved.

I never knew I was poor until I came to Canada and someone told me I was poor. Back in our tiny Croatian village, we all lived the same way, so nobody was "poor." We were all average or normal or some other description. Which proves that no one in life can make you feel something until you let them. We may not have had much money, but I was never poor in my mind. Poverty is temporary, something I believed I would rise above. It was simply a period in time.

Growing up with the sense that I was loved and supported has influenced me and helped me succeed in life. When others expect great things from you and make it clear that their support is lifelong and unconditional, you tend to expect great things of yourself.

> **"When others expect great things from you and make it clear that their support is lifelong and unconditional, you tend to expect great things of yourself."**

Making things real for my daughter

In 2010, I returned to Zbjeg with my daughter Caprice, who was 10 years old at the time. She and my other children had heard me talk about growing up in this poor village and arriving in Canada with almost nothing. But to my children, this was just a story, and stories are intangible. Sometimes they're not real at all, just a bunch of made-up events to prove a point. I wanted Caprice to understand that everything I had told her and her siblings about my childhood was true.

As we left Zagreb and drove down a country road through little towns and villages on the way to Zbjeg, I could see Caprice's expression change. Suddenly my past wasn't just a story. The centuries-old houses and barns, the farmyards and the people in the fields, they were all real.

Relatives who still lived in the same house as they did when I lived in Zbjeg greeted us warmly. I was almost disappointed to discover that the dirt floor in the house where I grew up had been replaced with sparkling tile. There was still no indoor bathroom, however, and Caprice's experience of the outhouse was, shall we say, enlightening.

Along with telling tales of my early childhood in Zbjeg, I had emphasized to all the children that they could do anything they set their minds to; they could become as big a success at whatever goal they set for themselves if they cared enough and worked hard enough to succeed. I think they believed me, but I suspect they felt a bit of skepticism about stories of my own beginnings.

Caprice has spent virtually all of her life in a very large house. Every day she shares and enjoys the things in life that I have managed to provide for her and her brother and sister. That is her reality, a reality so far removed from my childhood experience, both in Croatia and during my first years in Canada, that mine almost appears to be fiction.

Living among pigs, cows and chickens, and making treks through the dark to reach the outhouse, represented the starting points in my life. Caprice's starting point, where her life's journey began, is obviously very different. Our trip to Zbjeg showed her my starting point, and seeing where I came from gave her an immediate sense of how far I had travelled. Along with tangible proof of the tales I had been telling her came a measure of the journey I have taken to this point.

My children, Caprice, Skye and Brendan, can set their own directions and chart their own destinations with confidence. They understand that it can be done, and they know that their mother and father have total belief in their abilities. That's what helped me travel the distance I came—love from others, and confidence in myself.

The only way my children could disappoint me

It's not my intention to ensure that my children achieve the same level of success as I did, or even pursue a career in business. I want only to sell them on the vision of becoming the best that they can be, whatever path they choose to follow. None of this, I need to say, has anything to do with financial success. Will I be pleased if they achieve wealth like mine on their own? Of course I will. Will I be disappointed if they don't? Not a bit.

The only way my children would disappoint me would be by disappointing themselves by not fulfilling their dreams and exploring the boundaries of their talents.

The biggest tragedy in life is failing to reach your potential.

Achieving everything that their ambitions and abilities permit them to accomplish is all that Diane and I hope for our children, along with as much happiness as they can bear. You cannot ask for more from your children than that, nor can you ask more from yourself.

39

Adam's Dream and My Reality

As much as all parents try to teach values to their kids, they eventually discover that children have a good deal to teach parents as well. The most dramatic example of this occurred during my first summer of racing in the Ferrari Challenge series.

When I found myself with some extra time on the hot-lap schedule that year, I remembered a friend who works with children who have been stricken with cancer. He told me of a 15-year-old boy battling the disease who had always dreamed of riding in a Ferrari. I thought, why not offer this boy more than just a ride around the block in a Ferrari? Why not give him the experience of roaring down the racetrack, strapped in the passenger seat of my 458, making hairpin turns and sweeping around curves, the engine roaring in his ears? How cool would that be?

The boy's name was Adam, and he was very ill. He had been in the hospital for four years. When I made the offer to Adam and his parents, they accepted with enthusiasm. I was surprised to learn that he was so sick he had to travel from the hospital to the track in an ambulance. He was very frail at this point, but my worry for him subsided for a moment at the sight of the broad smile he flashed at me when he first saw the Ferrari race car.

Still, I had serious concerns. Among his complications was the need for special care because he had a hole in his chest where drugs were administered. All of this made me very cautious, even to the point of wondering if this had been such a good idea after all. Travelling at speed in a Ferrari is thrilling, but it is not the most comfortable ride in the world, even on the well-paved race-track used for the Toronto Indy. At racing speeds you are bounced around like a rag doll, and the G-force during turns and while accelerating and braking is substantial. *Maybe I better take it slow and easy,* I thought, as Adam was placed in the passenger seat next to me. But as soon as he was strapped in and the door closed, he leaned toward me and said, "I want to go really, really fast!"

That was all the incentive I needed. I don't think I took a faster hot lap that day, and the grin that came over Adam's face the moment I released the clutch in first gear was still there when I pulled back into the starting area after completing the circuit. The only person emotionally higher than Adam when we finished the lap was me, and I realized that no matter what may have occurred in my life, I had nothing to feel down about. I have countless reasons to be happy, and I need to remind myself of this from time to time. I also believe deeply in the concept of being in the moment—of experiencing to the fullest everything that is occurring to you and around you, and absorbing it with every sense of your body. No one can understand this more than someone with a limited time to live. And no one, I am convinced, can experience this aspect of life, this seizing of the moment, as fully as a child with a terminal ailment.

More pain than I could imagine

Adam helped me realize all the reasons I have to be happy and satisfied with my life. So did a short conversation I had with his parents a few moments later. His mother and father were grateful that Adam had had the chance to fulfil a dream. His mother told me she was a fan of mine, and asked the secret of my success. I replied without thinking, "Bad stuff happens in life, and when it does, you just have to get up the next day and carry on."

> "Bad stuff happens in life, and when it does, you just have to get up the next day and carry on."

My words brought a small sad smile to her face, and she said, "Yes, I know."

Immediately, I felt an inch high. Maybe less.

This woman woke up one day to learn that her son had an especially virulent form of cancer, and she and her family would face years of treatment, pain, heartbreak and distress. She would never see her son grow up, graduate from school, launch a career, choose a life partner or give her a grandchild. None of this was going to happen. She didn't need me to talk about resilience and courage. She and her husband and their son drew on more resilience and courage each day than I could imagine.

She knew I hadn't meant to dismiss her family's suffering with my remark, but I felt I owed her an apology anyway.

Adam and his parents reminded me that everything we do in

> " Both the death of Adam and the death of my father a few months earlier brought one word to my mind. The word has nothing to do with loss or mourning or even the passage of time. The word is simply: *Go!*"

life is subject to forces we cannot control. Knowing this shouldn't depress us. It should make us more determined than ever to seek and enjoy all the happiness we can gather around us. It should remind us, as Adam reminded me, of the window of time each of us is granted, and the realization that we never know when that window will close.

Adam died the spring after our ride on the racetrack. We all leave legacies behind, including those who pass on at such a terribly young age. The legacy that Adam left me were those seven words—"I want to go really, really fast!"—and the memory of the smile he wore all through the ride in a Ferrari going "really, really fast!"

Both the death of Adam and the death of my father a few months earlier brought one word to my mind. The word has nothing to do with loss or mourning or even the passage of time.

The word is simply: *Go!*

I have been going, to use Adam's phrase, "really, really fast" since the day I decided that I would work only for myself, building a company large enough and successful enough to provide careers for others, so that we could all share in the success.

So far it has been an amazing journey, with surprises popping up at every bend in the road. My business success and my participation on *Dragons' Den* and *Shark Tank* carried me to new destinations, as did my determination to win every race I enter in the Ferrari Challenge series.

When people I meet ask if I'm travelling as fast as ever, I confirm that I am.

No one so far has asked where I am going. If they should, my answer would be: "Wherever I need to be."

Acknowledgements

This book could not have happened without the talent and dedication of my co-author, John Lawrence Reynolds. I cannot think of a nicer person to spend a year with while discussing and expressing my views and values . . . and sharing the necessary quantities of Tim Hortons coffee.

I also owe a debt of gratitude to the team at HarperCollins Canada, first for convincing me that a second book was warranted, and second by applying their exceptional collective skills to make it happen. Jim Gifford's editorial guidance was once again invaluable, as were the contributions of Noelle Zitzer and Allegra Robinson.

My agents, Bruce Westwood and Carolyn Forde, provided critical advice and guidance in shaping the book and ensuring that it measured up to their own high standards. And I must acknowledge the members of the Herjavec Group, who, one way or another, proved or revealed so much of the material covered in this book—with special mention to Alena Oslopova for playing the difficult and often thankless role of traffic manager, gatekeeper and prompter.

April 2013